THE CRAFT OF PILLOW MAKING

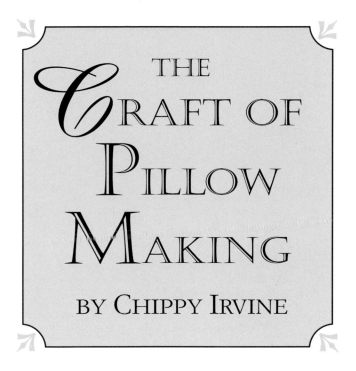

THE CRAFT OF PILLOW MAKING

BY CHIPPY IRVINE

PHOTOGRAPHS BY ALEX MCLEAN

CROWN TRADE PAPERBACKS
NEW YORK

Also by Chippy Irvine

The Farmhouse

The Townhouse

Second Homes

Private New York

Brunschwig & Fils Style (with Murray Douglas)

Copyright © 1996 by Chippy Irvine

Published by Crown Trade Paperbacks, Inc., 201 East 50th Street, New York, New York 10022. Member of the Crown Publishing Group.

Random House, Inc. New York, Toronto, London, Sydney, Auckland

CROWN TRADE PAPERBACKS and colophon are trademarks of Crown Publishers, Inc.

Printed in Hong Kong

Design by Lauren Dong

Library of Congress Cataloging-in-Publication Data
Irvine, Chippy.
The craft of pillow making / by Chippy Irvine.
Includes index.
1. Pillows. I. Title.

TT410.I78	1996
646.2'1-dc20	95-31105
	CIP

ISBN 0-517-88249-3

10 9 8 7 6 5 4 3 2 1

First Edition

THIS BOOK

IS DEDICATED TO MY DAUGHTERS,

EMMA AND JASSY.

CONTENTS

FOREWORD

My earliest memory of a cushion is of always having to sit on a recamier settee at my grandparents' farmhouse in Cumberland, England. The settee was upholstered in dark gray horsehair—slippery like a seal's coat—and as I always seemed to slip slowly off the slithery seat, I would pull down one or two of the soft cushions propped decoratively against the back and anchor myself with them. This was much disapproved of, when noticed, as these cushions were of great value. Hideous they seemed to me—awful silk moirés and brocades all overlaid and bordered—my grandmother had rather naughtily had them made up out of my grandfather's "put away" masonic aprons and stoles.

As Chippy has explained in her history and background to this book, these cloth cases with their soft stuffing have been a part of man's history for centuries, from ancient Egypt through the "mossy bank" of Shakespeare's Titania and the pillow Othello used as a murder weapon all the way to Doris Day's Technicolor *Pillow Talk.*

In my forty years as a decorator both in Europe and in America, decorative pillows have played a strong and continual element in all my work. I first realized their magic import from my mentor, the great John Fowler. He opened my eyes to all the possibilities of different fabrics, trims, and shapes. As I worked with him on many varied projects and fabulous historic houses, I began to understand how decorating schemes for a house develop room by room, adding furniture piece by piece. I realized that intriguing cushions in a finished room are the costume jewelry of haut décor. Once the background and furniture are all perfect and correct, ingenious pillows set off and highlight all the magic.

When I started my own decorating business in New York, nearly all my first jobs were ones that had great financial restrictions, and where successful solutions were mostly achieved by rearranging existing furniture (which clients could not afford to recover) and then spiking the whole space with inexpensive but brilliant cushions. The cushions led to better and better jobs, and by the end of our first decade, my partner, Tom Fleming, and I had risen to a point when Mrs. Averell Harriman in Washington—recommending us to Katherine Graham—remarked "Do *everything* Keith suggests, but okay only half the number of cushions he proposes!"

You will find this book an inspiration and stimulus to explore the possibilities of pillow making, which will add exciting highlights to your own life and home.

Keith B. Irvine

Overleaf: Equipment needed for pillow making can be found in most households where sewing is done. On a cutting table, clockwise from top left, are a metal right-angled ruler, pinking shears, piping cords, a sewing box containing some covered piping, a basket of threads, a sewing machine with a box of machine spools and a zipper foot, scissors, a pincushion, a thimble, weights, and a tape measure.

INTRODUCTION

Pillows have always been elegant furnishings. They have a subliminal effect around the home, giving one a feeling of comfort and ease with a suggestion of luxury. Pillows have been the decoration of choice far longer than upholstered furniture (the earliest cited example of upholstery dates from the time of Henry VII in England and it is an upholstered sofa still to be seen at Knole in Kent). There are, however, ancient Egyptian tomb paintings of pillows that were probably stuffed with down from the many geese depicted in these delightful illustrations. Seat pads were also prevalent throughout history. In fact, a beaded hassock was found among the treasures of Tutankhamen's tomb. The ancient Greeks and Romans used cushions to soften the seats of their leather slung chairs.

Closer to our own times, pillows have not only been used for comfort but have found a place in history and literature. In 1603, Queen Elizabeth I of England tried to forestall death by refusing to get into her bed, where she was convinced she would die, and she actually died on a pile of pillows on the floor. The following year, Shakespeare wrote *Othello,* in which a pillow played a dramatic part, when Othello used it in a jealous rage to stifle the beautiful Desdemona. Like so many of Shakespeare's plays, the source of the tragedy was much earlier, being based on a tale in Cinthio's *Hecatommithi,* written in 1565.

Artists have featured pillows in paintings, too. Dutch interiors of the seventeenth century—such as Franken's rendering of a room in Rubens's house—show elaborately woven tapestry pillows.

In the eighteenth century, François Boucher painted *Miss O'Brien,* with a woman pinkly naked and wallowing in a sea of pillows. It can be seen at The Frick Collection in New York City.

Early-nineteenth-century "Oriental"—or Middle Eastern harem scenes—were scattered with exotic tasseled cushions, to inspire, a century later, the Bakst decors of the Ballet Russes. These scenes in turn induced couturier Paul Poiret to flights of fancy with patterned or shirred or cylindrical and spherical betasseled cushions when he opened a school for young decorators. They sold their products under the label Martine, named after Poiret's daughter.

The Duchess of Windsor is reputed to have started the vogue for placing needlepoint pillows along the back of sofas. When crossing the Atlantic on the Cunard *Queens,* the great steamship named after royalty, in the 1930s, she would take her favorite bibelots to accessorize her cabin suites, including just the right pillows.

In much the same way, today many fashion designers—such as Ralph Lauren and Laura Ashley—have added home decoration to their businesses with lines of pillows, fabrics, and furnishings.

WHY MAKE PILLOWS?

Pillows, especially sumptuous, rich-looking ones, plumped enticingly on a sofa, are often the first things you notice in a room.

According to many professional decorators, the quickest, most effective, and not too expensive way to give a room a face-lift is to rearrange the existing furniture and then add some spectacular pillows. You can do the same thing, and your friends will be amazed at the boost these fun-to-make pillows will give to your living space.

Pillows, fortunately, are fairly easy projects for the novice to tackle. Put simply, you cut a square of fabric, stitch and turn it, stuff it with something, and there you are. The great bonus is that pillows do not consume yards and yards of cloth like slipcovers or curtains, yet just a few unique cushions in carefully chosen colors can instantly transform a whole room.

How is it, then, that quality pillows are so expensive to buy? And how come the beautiful cushions designed by decorators look so much more luxurious than standard department store offerings?

Here in this book are the answers, and plenty of hints to guide you through making your own truly elegant and enticing pillows, custom-colored to enhance your own decor and your own whims.

The following pages will take you step by step through the process of making a perfect pillow. Starting with a basic square, you will learn how to cut the shape accurately, how to make sure the corners don't stick out like rabbit's ears, how to cut and stitch bias piping from your own fabric, and how to assemble the pillow.

Chapter 2 will describe which kinds of fabrics make the best cushions and what are the most appropriate trimmings—braids, pipings, ribbons, and cords—to use with them for various settings. Also you will discover what stuffings are available and their advantages and disadvantages so that you can use the appropriate filling.

In subsequent chapters you will learn the techniques of making the softened French corners needed on certain pillows, how to apply ruffles and flanges of many varieties, and how to mount antique needlepoint and "frame" it on a cushion so as to enhance its beauty. The book is rich with design ideas, from producing a sophisticated pillow by cleverly mitering a simple stripe, to creating a masculine cushion from a piece of antique carpet-

ing, to making frothy, lacy pillows for the boudoir.

Pillows come not only in many sizes but also in many shapes. An antique embroidered bellpull—useless in today's world in its original form—if mounted correctly might be perfect transformed into a narrow, oblong pillow for a fireside bench. You may have a yen for the shirred circular taffeta cushions popular in the 1930s, or for sleek, spherical art deco velvet pillows.

Needlepoint intended for fire screens can be mounted onto the most elegant, shield-shaped pillows. Treasured antique scraps or pieces of Grandmother's wedding dress can be transformed into pillows that can be seen and enjoyed every day. A quilt that has seen better days—but which you hate to part with—can be cut into cushions. I know of a Dior ball gown that was made into ravishingly chic pillows.

Almost no scrap is too small. Tiny, beautifully made pillows can look as delightful as big ones. This book will describe how to outline your scrap with a piping that brings out its "life," mount it on a complementary-colored fabric, edge the pillow with a wider piping, and back the whole thing with yet another fabric. This "mounting" technique echoes the way subtle watercolors and engravings are enhanced by professional framers using refined French matting.

Perhaps you have some cane-seated chairs that need the protection of seat pads? You will learn how to make a template, or pattern, so that the pad will fit the seat precisely, and how to sew ties to the corners so that they cannot slip out of place. Some chairs have cane backs, and for these, shaped lambrequins can be made, with ties at the back to slot through the canework. Some seat pads need to be thin as a pancake, with a single piece of piping around the edge for definition. Others may be thick as a club sandwich with piping at the top and bottom edges.

You can also send delightful presents via pillows. Exquisite heart-shaped pillows make wonderful Valentine gifts. Children love to get personalized "tooth fairy" pillows. You can paint pillows (painting on velvet was a craft popular among Victorian ladies) to make your pillows truly unique, and at the same time pick your own colors. You can embroider special messages, applique designs, interweave ribbons. You will find any number of ideas for your living room, den, bedroom, children's rooms, and friends' rooms.

All of these ideas are merely that . . . ideas! They are not intended as projects to be slavishly copied, but rather as inspirations to set the imagination going. Everyone has different needs, tastes, and materials at hand. Discover your own style rather than merely copying others'. Learn to use your eye; collect references—such as magazine clippings that give you ideas and scraps that attract you. When you put together your own fabric and color combinations, you will find that you have created something entirely individual.

Throughout the book, diagrams illustrate basic cutting and sewing techniques. By following these you can save time and produce well-made, professional-looking pillows. But the design of your cushions should be yours alone! Lavish photographs of the finished cushions, many in their own stylish locations, may pique the imagination. There's no need to be bored by taking the easy way and lining up a row of matching pillows on a sofa. Chapter 9 illustrates how a professional designer logically arranges an interesting variety of pillows by size, pattern, and color to bring the whole room into balance. At the illustrious English decorating firm Colefax & Fowler, John Fowler—often considered the high priest of decorating—once spent a whole hour explaining to an assistant how to puff up, dress down, and properly place a *cushion* (as pillows are always referred to in England; *pillows,* the British say, are for the bed).

At the end of the book is a list of Sources and Suppliers for decorative fabrics. Many of these firms sell only "to the trade," which means the goods have to be bought through an architect or a decorator. However, there are many warehouse and discount operations where short runs of quality decorative fabrics can be found. Sources for unusual trimmings are included, and also antiques shops and businesses that specialize in vintage fabrics, household linens, and laces. The names of firms that supply upholstery items from which you can buy stuffings, muslin, pillow ticking, and various widths of fillers for piping are listed.

Perhaps the very first pillow was a mossy knoll in the Garden of Eden. *The Craft of Pillow Making* should help you to visualize, then create your own earthly paradise.

CHAPTER 1

EQUIPMENT

Most of the tools needed to make pillows can be found in any home where sewing is done. A sewing machine is required, together with the skill to use it, though pillows can be—sometimes must be—hand-stitched. Essential and optional equipment needed to create your own pillows is described below.

CUTTING TABLE

The average household does not own a cutting table. Many home stitchers have to cut out on the dining room table, or the kitchen table, or the floor. Pillows are smaller than curtains, bed-spreads, or dresses, so they can be more easily cut on small, makeshift surfaces. A lightweight, fold-away aluminum table found in hardware stores is useful as a cutting table in a small apartment. Placing two together is even better, giving ample cutting space. In my workroom, a carpenter made a vinyl-topped cutting table, hinged so it can be folded up against the wall with the legs tucked into it when not in use. Foldaway card tables can be used, with larger tops fitted onto them when needed for cutting larger items.

FABRIC

See "Materials and Stuffings," page 9.

IRON AND IRONING BOARD

Most households have an iron and an ironing board. Professional seamstresses often use power-ful steam irons that are turned on at the beginning of the working day and not turned off until going-home time. (Seamstresses often heat their lunch sandwiches against the steam iron!) To run an iron all day is inefficient in the average household unless it is in continual use. A regular steam iron is useful, however, because it can remove wrinkles caused by fabric folds.

Another way to remove wrinkles is to hold the fabric over a kettle of boiling water, but be careful not to scald your fingers. Pressing the fabric with a damp cloth is yet another alternative. Because pillows are not usually very large, an ironing board is not absolutely essential. You can place padding on a kitchen table and use that instead.

A needle board, used to press velvet or velveteen, is useful. Needle boards are made up of tiny upright wires set on a thick rubbery canvas back. You can press velvet directly onto the needle board without bruising the pile. If you do not have a needle board, you can stand the steam iron on its end and pull the wrong side of the velvet against the iron, letting the steam lift the pile, or you can hold the velvet over boiling water.

MARKING TOOLS

Professional cutters use tailor's chalk or tailor's wax to draw shapes on fabric to be cut. Chalk comes in slender white or red oblongs which can be sharpened with the blade of a pair of scissors to keep the line fine. Tailors' wax comes in white, black, and yellow, and can also be sharpened. A well-sharpened pencil or a contrasting-colored

5

pencil can be used instead of tailors' chalk or wax. Mark the fabric on the wrong side whenever possible, just in case you make a mistake and the mark cannot be erased. An exception to this rule would be if you are using a printed fabric that has to be carefully placed on the pillow and the pattern cannot be discerned from the wrong side.

PILLOW INTERIORS

See Stuffings on page 25.

PINS

Always have plenty of clean, sharp pins. Professional seamstresses often wind thick fabric around the body of the sewing machine in which to keep pins while they are sewing. Sew a wide elastic band onto a regular strawberry-shaped pincushion so it can be worn on the wrist to keep pins always handy. Never hold pins in your mouth!

PIPING CORD AND FILLERS

Piping filler cord of various widths ranging from $\frac{1}{8}$ inch to 1 inch (3 mm to 3 cm) in diameter can be found in craft shops and upholstery supply shops. For very thin piping you can use one strand or several strands of household cotton string. The thickness needed depends on the design of the pillow. Prefabricated piping in a limited range of colors can be bought from upholstery supply stores, but it is usually sold in packages rather than in small amounts by the yard.

RULERS

A metal right-angled ruler is useful for cutting pillows accurately. This type of ruler is 24 inches long and 2 inches wide on one arm, and 16 inches long and $1\frac{1}{2}$ inches wide on the other arm, which is at a right angle to the first.

In a pinch, a right angle can be established by setting anything rectangular, such as a book or magazine, against the selvedge and drawing a horizontal line along it. A wooden yardstick is best for cutting

piping yardage. Make sure it is perfectly straight; with age, wooden rulers tend to warp. A 12-inch ruler and a protractor are useful but not essential.

SCISSORS AND SHEARS

Professionals have two pairs: one small pair kept next to the sewing machine to clip threads and make tiny notches, and one large pair to cut fabric. You can get by with one medium pair of scissors. Make sure they are sharpened periodically. There are few things more frustrating than trying to cut fabric with dull scissors.

Pinking shears may be needed for certain pillows, such as felt pillows with pinked flanges or taffeta pillows with double-bias-shirred ruffles with pinked edges.

SEWING MACHINE

A sewing machine is essential, but almost any regular sewing machine can be used to make pillows. It does not have to be the latest state-of-the-art model. I still use a Singer machine I was given on my twenty-first birthday, a weighty, all-steel, perfectly usable machine that looks very old-fashioned nowadays. However, it does the job as well if not better than many of the lightweight plastic machines of today. My sister in England is still using our grandmother's hand-turned machine with its long, thin, cylindrical bobbins!

Professional seamstresses use factory machines engineered to run very fast. They are wonderful to use if you are skilled and not intimidated by their speed and power.

SEWING MACHINE NEEDLES

Always have on hand various weights of sewing machine needles. You will probably use a size 14 needle—the average size—most of the time, but sometimes you will be using layers of heavy furnishing fabric together with bulky cording, and your sewing machine may balk at the thickness, especially where heavy cordings overlap. For heavyweight fabric always use a heavyweight size

16 needle. If that needle breaks, consider hand-stitching the thickest parts as an alternative to machine-stitching. A size 12, which is a fine needle, is best for lacy boudoir pillows.

SEWING NEEDLES

One side of a pillow is stitched up by hand, so the same advice applies for sewing needles: Have on hand several sizes and weights. When making pillows of fur or leather, use leather needles. These are specially sharpened to cut through the skin while stitching. Sometimes curved upholstery needles are necessary for pillows made of heavy rugs. Heavy straight upholstery needles are needed for tufted pillows, those held by buttons, bows, or rosettes.

To repair needlepoint, use appropriately sized needlepoint needles that do not have sharp points. To repair beadwork on antique embroidery, use the very fine beading needles that are slender enough to go through the holes in tiny beads.

TAPE MEASURE

Every household should have a tape measure of some sort. For sewing, use a standard fabric tape measure with inches on one side and centimeters on the other. Replace old tape measures because they become inaccurate when worn.

THIMBLE

Professional seamstresses *always* wear thimbles for hand sewing. Find one that fits and get used to wearing it—or you will wear out the end of your middle finger.

THREAD

In a professional workroom there are many shades of thread to choose from. Upholstery workrooms usually use heavier thread than that used in making clothing. The average household is far more stringent. It pays to match your threads accurately because you will often have to topstitch or sink a stitch close to the piping. The glamour of your pillow will be lost if the thread is mismatched. If you need to use thicker thread for strength or for an effect, use double thread. Buy an extra spool, and run one spool from the top of the machine and the second from the vertical spindle used to hold the spool when it is winding thread onto the bobbin. Thread the machine using both strands as if one, and thread the needle with both. The bobbin underneath will be a single thread.

WEIGHTS

These are needed to hold doubled cloth in place when cutting. Though professional workrooms use metal weights, many other objects will do, such as large smooth stones, books, or heavy paperweights.

ZIPPERS

Not all pillows need zippers; indeed, the more luxurious ones are cheapened by the mundane look of a zipper. Antique fabric pillows look wrong with modern zippers.

However, zippers make sense on pillows that have to be washed or cleaned frequently. They are also useful on pillows in children's rooms. They should be used on canvas outdoor pillows, provided the zippers are washable plastic. Metal zippers are strong, but tend to rust and jam if used outside.

Zippers are essential on cushions (seat pads) used for armchair and sofa slipcovers so that they can be easily removed and cleaned. These zippers are often made of metal and are of upholstery weight. They are available in limited colors and sizes.

ZIPPER FOOT

A zipper foot is an *absolute* essential, necessary for making piping as well as setting a zipper, because it enables the machine needle to stitch right up close to the piping cord. Some zipper feet are adjustable and can be used on the right or the left side of the zipper or piping. Others can be purchased either left or right.

CHAPTER 2
MATERIALS AND STUFFINGS

Ever since I was a child I have been fascinated by textiles and have always kept a "rag bag" for interesting fabric scraps. At first, the scraps were tiny and used mostly to make dolls' clothes. Now the scraps are bigger, more numerous, and require far more space and organization. Rarely is anything thrown out. I keep pieces of fabric and trimmings in boxes, cupboards, and drawers in the attic according to color so that I can draw upon this library of remnants frequently when making pillows.

Not everyone has the luxury of a sewing room or an attic to keep scraps of cloth. Fabrics and trimmings may have to be specially purchased each time that one or several pillows are to be made. Happily, pillows do not require large amounts of fabric, but the selection of fabric is important because pillows can effect a dramatic change in the look of a room.

When looking for fabric, always carry color references such as a swatch of curtain material, a tiny piece of carpeting, a fragment of wallpaper, paint chips, or perhaps an inspiring magazine photograph.

Where you shop for fabric depends on where you live. In big cities there are many choices. The most wonderful selections are in the decorator and design fabrics houses, many of which sell to the trade only. (See "Sources and Suppliers," page 103). These fabrics can be bought often only through an interior designer or architect, or with a resale number. Some fabric houses are very strict about this rule, so be prepared to be barred at the door. Others are becoming more lenient, or have retail divisions. In Europe the rules are somewhat different and most fabric houses are prepared to sell at retail prices to anyone who walks in.

In some areas there are discount houses that sell odd amounts and closeouts of decorative fabrics. As huge amounts of yardage are not needed, you can often find a bargain, but be sure it is a fabric that really catches your fancy.

Also try retail dress-fabric stores—but be warned that fabrics made for clothing are often lighter in weight and may have to be backed. Fashion fabrics also tend to be in the current colors and patterns, which will obviously date them. For the most desirable cushions, select classic—but not dull—traditional patterns and weaves, not today's fads. Dress fabrics also tend to have a high content of man-made fibers such as polyester, nylon, or rayon to make them washable and less expensive—and tend to look it!

For one-of-a-kind vintage fabrics, search thrift shops. You may find interesting secondhand clothes that can be ripped apart and recycled as pillows, or quilts that are threadbare in places but have usable good areas. When shopping at either ritzy antiques

Small pieces of fabrics suitable for making into pillows can be sorted into piles to form a library of colors that can be seen at a glance.

shops or open market stalls, watch out for that special piece of cloth or ribbon, a commemorative handkerchief, a remnant of silk damask, a badge from a worn-out blazer, or a scrap of antique needlepoint that can become a wonderful pillow. And be sure to buy the remnant there and then if you fall in love with it, or you will regret it later.

One of the great things about antique and vintage textiles is that they are usually made of natural fibers: silk, linen, metallic threads, and cotton. Occasionally you will come across wool remnants or garments, but old wool has a difficult time surviving the onslaughts of moths.

With modern technology, many decorative fabric companies sell fabrics made of natural fibers blended with a proportion of man-made fibers for strength, washability, and price. These blends can be practical and beautiful. Polyester, though it has its uses, is not always distinguished looking, nor really all that practical because stains seem to imbed themselves forever in polyester. Be warned also against knitted fabrics, which, unless brilliantly and creatively handled, tend to look cheap.

The following list describes how certain fabrics can best be used in making pillows. Descriptions of textiles can be found in "Glossary of Terms," at the end of the book.

FORMAL AND LUXURIOUS FABRICS

The most glamorous fabrics are made of silk, which has a soft, pearly sheen and responds to color better than any other fiber. Many decorative fabrics have a proportion of silk to give luster and color, though other fibers may be incorporated as backing or filler to give body. Pure silk fabrics used in decoration are very expensive.

Fabrics that make some of the best-looking pillows are brocaded silk, damask, ottoman, moiré, satin, taffeta, and velvet. These are all technically weaves, and all the above can be made in silk, cotton, and other fibers. Be warned that some fabrics in the wrong setting can look *too* opulent, especially moiré, satin, and cut velvet.

BROCADED SILK

I once made pillows from the remains of an eighteenth-century bishop's robe of elaborately brocaded French silk. The design was utterly secular—flowers and garlands in persimmon, russet, rose, and cream with cornucopias of somewhat tarnished silver and gold threads, all on a sky blue ground. It seemed a shame to tuck the pieces of cloth away in a drawer unseen and unenjoyed. The best parts made large pillows and the tiny pieces were formed into doll-sized pillows. Not a scrap was wasted. Even the hand-sewn lining of the robe, a soft blue-green strié silk too fragile for a pillow, is still in use as a bedroom table skirt.

Brocading is a form of weaving with an embroidered look (not strictly speaking a fabric or fiber, though fabrics are often referred to as brocade). A *lampas* has a similar look but is of heavier weight. Whether you use brocaded silk that is antique or newly produced, it is a glamorous fabric for pillows.

DAMASK

Damask can be made of cotton, linen, rayon, silk, or a combination of these fibers. It is perennially used for household linen, but is also currently popular in decoration because it is hard-wearing and has an easily accepted monotone surface texture. A pair of simple, pure silk damask pillows can look luxurious and perfectly at home on a well-dressed sofa.

GROSGRAIN

Though known better as a ribbon, grosgrain is also a fabric, ribbed and silky, and it is useful for making formal-looking pillows. The ribs are smaller in scale than ottoman.

GROS POINT AND PETIT POINT

Though gros point and petit point are both known as stitches in needlepoint embroidery (see Needlepoint on page 19), there are decorative fabrics by those names that imitate needlepoint and come in several colorings. Both are useful as framing fabrics for antique needlepoint or as backing for needlepoint pillows.

MOIRÉ

Moiré's distinctive watered look can work for pillows in very formal rooms, but also tends to look a bit gussied up. A small amount, used for framing if it is the desired color, is fine.

OTTOMAN

This horizontally ribbed fabric is one of the most effective for pillow making. Ottoman can be used in combination with other fabrics, such as for framing antique needlepoint or as backing for a pillow. It is especially effective as piping fabric because the ribs, when on the bias needed for piping, form a cordlike texture.

SATIN

Satin can be made of many fibers, but is most lustrous when of silk. Heavy furnishing silk satin is one of the most beautiful fabrics for a simple pillow, needing little more than a great-quality goose down interior, and perhaps an edging of moss fringe. (See the coral satin pillow on the sofa on page 100, and the seat pad on page 101.)

All the major furnishing textile houses have versions of satin weave fabrics. Heavy furnishing satin can be striped in colors or woven in monotone satin and ottoman stripes, or strié to give a grainy surface effect. There are many combinations of weaves and colors.

Antique or vintage heavy satin—sometimes called slipper satin because the weight is heavy enough to use for shoes—is often used for wedding gowns. You might come across just such a dress and make wonderful creamy pillows from it.

Be aware that heavy furnishing-weight satin tends to curl back on itself, making it bothersome to cut. A tiny strip of adhesive tape stuck along the wrong side and plenty of weights to hold the cloth will help. Once the pillow is finished, the effect is beautiful and well worthwhile. Make sure that you

have smooth fingernails when using satin or any precious silky fabrics; any roughness can snag.

Satin is also made in light dress weights, usually in rayon or polyester, but is not as successful for pillows except as a base for lacy boudoir ones.

STRIÉ SATIN

Strié (streaked) furnishing cotton in a satin weave is effective because it has an interesting but not overpowering surface design and combines particularly successfully with vintage fabrics.

TAFFETA

Taffeta is lighter in weight than satin or ottoman, and because of this responds well to shirring techniques such as ruched piping (see the photograph on page 38), French—or Turkish—corners (see pages 16 and 30), gathered ruffles (see page 43), or circular gathered pillows (see the bottom-right photograph on page 83.)

Taffeta can be made of silk, synthetics, and cotton. Colors are most lively when the taffeta is silk, though there are some good-looking synthetic taffetas. Taffeta is a formal, precious-looking fabric that makes wonderful, lightweight, soft-as-thistledown pillows. For more informal, less-delicate pillows, cotton taffeta can be used and is available in many colors. (See *taffeta* in "Glossary of Terms" for variations.)

VELVET

Silk velvet has a thick, erect pile that can be bruised easily. The backing is often cotton or rayon. Silk velvet takes color beautifully and makes magnificent pillows, whether plain or embellished.

When cutting velvet, be aware of the direction of the pile. Look carefully at the velvet from all directions, for the surface color varies according to your view. Stroke the velvet. The smoother direction—the down pile—is usually lighter in color; the up-brushed pile usually looks richer. You have to decide which direction you prefer when cutting a pillow.

When cutting doubled-up velvet, do not lay the

Here is a selection of luxurious fabrics suitable for pillow making. Included are silk velvet, plush, cut velvet, plain and checked silk taffeta, striped moiré, heavy silk satin, and silk taffeta shot with metallic threads.

fabric face to face because the pile of one side will push the other, causing inaccurate cutting. Instead, lay velvet back to back. When stitching velvet on the wrong side with the two piles facing each other, pull each fabric taut to make sure the same pushing action does not take place, otherwise the slippage can be as much as an inch along the side of a pillow.

Velvet can be made of cotton, synthetics, or a combination of both and comes in many variations (see *velvet* in "Glossary of Terms"). Included in the following list are various pile fabrics that are not strictly speaking velvet, but have a similar plushy effect:

Antique velvet, *ciselé* velvet, *chenille, corduroy* (uncut corduroy has a ribless pile), *cut* velvet, *dévoré* velvet (used mainly for clothing as it is rather fragile, but can be used, backed with a firm fabric, for soft, cherished pillows that will not get tossed about a lot), *figured* velvet, *gaufrage, linen* velvet (which has a rugged, more sporty quality compared to the fine look of silk velvet, though it is a fiber that takes color almost as well as silk), *mohair* velvet (used mostly in decoration, and works well for pillows), *panne* velvet, *pile on pile* velvet, *voided* velvet, *plush, single* velvet (also sometimes called *wire* velvet), *velour* (which is also a knitted fabric used for sportswear, and to be used

for pillows only in desperation), *velveteen* (a versatile fabric for pillows, as it can look both formal and casual; it can be used to frame embroidery and to back pillows; it was chosen in the nineteenth century to make theorem paintings and today is still the ideal cloth to use for painted pillows [see Chapter 5]), and *voided* velvet.

We all are living increasingly informal lives and our furnishings reflect this trend. Many times we do not want the upkeep involved with luxurious surroundings. Indeed, the ultimate luxury may be not having to pay too much attention to our habitats and not worrying about damage. Homes are being simplified, but in elegant ways. Cotton is easy to care for, and can be wonderfully chic. Here are some fabrics for relaxed, contemporary pillows that can be right at home in many different settings.

PRINTS

ABSTRACTS

In some modern settings, floral or pictorial chintzes look out of place. More suitable might be abstract designs, haphazard patterns, or modernistic or art deco–inspired motifs, which can be neutral or colorful and are printed on a variety of base fabrics.

BATIK

Batik is a type of design that can be used in both a traditional, formal room or a casual, modern setting. Batiks have an exotic, ethnic look, but can be remarkably sophisticated, bringing subtle coloring into an interior design scheme.

CALICO

When we talk of calico now, we usually mean a cotton with a background color covered in simple, small-scale designs in two or three colors. Because the designs are usually simple flowers or geometrics with a distinctively naive, American country look, calico works well in informal spaces such as children's rooms, guest rooms, play rooms, and kitchens. Since they are inexpensive, calicos can be used in quantity, lending themselves to ruffles and patchwork. Calicos mix well, and many designs are available in retail and craft stores.

CHINTZ

This is a printed fabric generally used in interior decoration that can be either formal or casual, depending on the design and the way it is handled. Instead of being hand-painted like the original

A selection of neutrally toned fabrics includes small prints, stripes, checks, and textures. These combine well and can be used in country and casual settings.

Indian *chites,* chintz is now block-, screen-, or machine-printed. Even today however, the most subtle chintzes are still block-printed, though these are expensive because that process is slow.

One characteristic of chintz is its highly glazed surface, although the degree of glazing can vary. When chintz is made without a glazed finish, it is similar to a furnishing fabric called cretonne. Cretonne is usually made of cotton, but can also be linen or rayon.

Though chintzes began with Indian designs—exotic flowers, fruits, birds, and large "tree of life" designs surrounded by elaborate borders—many other designs with Chinese, Japanese, Middle Eastern, and European influences emerged. Floral designs usually come to mind at the mention of chintz, though there are many other designs available, from abstract to pictorial. Knowledgeable interior decorators recognize a handful of superb, traditional designs on chintz that flow in and out of fashion but will never die.

Many interior designers who, because of shifts in fashion would not consider upholstering whole pieces of furniture in chintz, like to use this colorful fabric for pillows as accents in an otherwise fairly neutral room. When the desire for more texture is fashionable, many classic chintz designs are printed on linen or linen blends, which is just as distinctive for use as pillows.

CONVERSATIONALS

Conversationals can have words, people, animals, vegetables, cartoons, objects, and scenes. Known as "theme" prints—such as teacups, hunting scenes, buildings, circus performers, kites, paw prints, you name it—they are generally used as accents. The use of this kind of print as both upholstery and curtains, for instance, might be too much. However, isolated as a pillow, a specific effect can be readily achieved.

GEOMETRICS

Geometrics such as triangles, circles, checks, and stripes can be useful as pillows that blend into a room rather than make bold statements. Geomet-

rics can work in masculine rooms as they are seldom threateningly overfeminine.

IKATS

Originally ikats were warp-printed fabrics. Ikat-inspired fabrics were extremely popular ethnic designs with a Middle Eastern flavor in the 1960s and 1970s, and were much imitated by machine or screen printing. A more sophisticated version of warp-printed fabric is chiné. In a casual room, ikat patterns are suitable for pillows, but in a formal salon or glamorous bedroom, a chiné would work best.

NEUTRALS

Neutrals are an important category for many people who are made a little nervous by color. There is a perception that color might jar, or be too feminine, and therefore there is comparative safety in beige. Keep your eyes open for neutral fabrics that have pattern and texture, such as a fine stripe, a fancy weave, or an almost imperceptible allover print.

PAISLEY

Nowadays most paisley designs are printed, though they were intricately woven when originally made in the Scottish town of Paisley. They come in any number of different colorings and fabrics—cotton, linen, challis, velveteen. Because paisleys are usually multicolored, they blend well into a design scheme when used for pillows. A classic combination for a living room might be a tartan carpet, a small-scale foulard for curtains, a small, simple windowpane check on the sofa, a paisley-slipcovered armchair, and paisley pillows on the sofa.

STRIPES

Stripes come in every fiber and many weights, sizes, colors, and combinations. They can be printed or woven. Pieced together, stripes can be mitered in many ways to make unusual pillows. Bear in mind that one-way, printed stripes take up a lot of yardage if they are mitered. (See Stripes, page 55.)

TINY FLORALS

As distinct from the tiny florals of calicos, there are many white or light-ground florals, monotone or multicolor, that can be used for pillows. Small, delicate florals are particularly suitable for bedrooms.

TOILE

Toile is a French word that has various meanings. In decorating terms, toile is a shortened form for toile de Jouy, generally used now to mean a fine, monotone scenic design printed on plain woven cotton.

Toiles are usually printed in black, red, green, or blue on a white or natural ground, but they can also be printed on colored grounds. I have sometimes found it necessary to dye a toile to create the right ground color for a pillow.

There are various classic toiles that depict scenes—such as the discovery of America, the invention of ballooning, bucolic scenes of the four seasons, and Sir Walter Scott's *The Lady of the Lake.*

Toiles make interesting pillows because they tell a story, but being monotone, they do not intrude on a room. If they need to be brought into a color scheme, contrasting piping can always be added to the pillows (see the photograph on page 16). There are some prints that have a toile effect from a distance, but in fact are more freely drawn versions of toiles, produced at a later date by screen or machine instead of by fine copperplate printing. These prints are not trying to be cheaper copies of the fine, engraved effect, but have a special quality of their own.

WOVENS

CANVAS

Canvas or duck can be given a water-resistant finish and used for outdoor pillows, cushions, and to cover the seats of banquette pads. Bear in mind that any colored canvas used outside will eventually fade. Always bring pillows indoors at night, for the fabric will get stained and moldy in damp air. Canvas can be printed or woven in striped patterns. These are sometimes called awning stripes. If needed for mitered pillows, use woven stripes because they look the same on both sides and are more economical to cut and match.

CHECKS

There are thousands of variations of checked fabric, made in every type of fiber. Some of these variations include: *houndstooth* check (sometimes called *dogtooth* check), like a four-pointed star; *district* check, a small houndstooth with an over plaid; *buffalo plaid,* a square, block plaid; and *windowpane* check, with open rectangles. Many of these designs work well in a masculine room such as a library or a boy's bedroom, or in a rugged country living room. (See the following pages for gingham and linen checks and for tartans.)

CHEVRON

This is another term for a *herringbone* weave. It can also apply to printed designs that form zigzag stripes. Chevron weaves can be found in many different fibers and blends, and, depending on the weight of the cloth, can be used for the body of a pillow or for trimming.

CHINO

The most usual colors are khaki or sand, but chino can be found in retail fabric stores in other colors too. As with denim (see below), chino garments can be recycled as pillows for an informal room.

DENIM

Some of the wittiest pillows have been made from denim, the most American of fabrics despite its French derivation. I have seen long, thin, cylindrical pillows made from the legs of jeans, tied at each end like a Christmas cracker, looking wonderful in a Montana fishing ranch; pillows with jean pockets, jacket pockets, and Western snappers on them;

embroidered denim pillows, even ruffled denim pillows. Everyone has access to denim, so use your imagination.

DIMITY

In decoration, dimity has a corded or striped effect. Furnishing dimity is a good pillow fabric as it gives surface interest to an otherwise white or solid-colored material.

DOBBY

A type of weave with a small repeating pattern, dobbies come in various fibers and weights and are useful for adding a small but unobtrusive texture or pattern to a pillow.

EYELET

Machine-made eyelet is available as beading (a narrow insertion through which ribbon may be threaded); as a galloon (a narrow edging with a finished scallop on either side); as ruffled edging; or as piece goods. All of these can be used to make or trim pillows that are suitable for a feminine bedroom.

GINGHAM

A staple for home seamstresses, gingham checks come in a variety of sizes, colors, and blends. They are inexpensive and are sold in many retail fabric stores. Use gingham for pillows in children's rooms or country settings. If the gingham you select is lightweight, reinforce the pillow body with sheeting. Gingham is ideal for ruffles.

In this breakfast room the seat pad and pillows with French corners and plain blue piped edges (echoing the plates on the wall) are covered in a toile based on the story of Sir Walter Scott's *The Lady of the Lake,* a novel that was popular during the first half of the nineteenth century.

Here is a selection of washable cotton fabrics suitable for making into pillows.

LINEN

Though many of the fabrics described above and below may be made of linen or linen blends, it is worthwhile noting some special characteristics of linen: Linen responds to color almost as brilliantly as silk—it is virtually impossible to find an ugly-colored linen; linen runs from lightweight, often called handkerchief linen, to very heavy, slubbed fabric; linen can be printed, though because of its texture, printing is never as sharp as on cotton; and linen is often woven into checks and stripes and other fancy patterns. There is a distinctive linen gingham-style check, about ½ inch (13 mm) in size, that is used traditionally in decoration on the back of upholstered wood-framed chairs, ones that will have a much fancier fabric on the front. These linen checks are usually in neutral colors. Down-filled and large, they make good-looking, nonaggressive pillows that can mingle with almost anything. (See the section on Velvet on pages 11–12 for linen velvet.)

MADRAS

Madras comes in a variety of checks, plaids, and stripes. Sometimes madras is made up as patchwork. Madras combines well with denim. Use it for pillows in a casual setting.

MUSLIN

In pillow making, muslin is useful as backing, or to try out an idea. With a good commercial finish on the cloth, muslin can be used in many ways: embroidered, smocked, ruffled, tucked, shirred, and generally embellished. It can also be dyed. Muslin has a casual, cottony, informal look.

PIQUÉ

Piqué is most typically a pure white fabric, but it can be piece-dyed any color. Because it is wonderfully washable, a deeply sculpted piqué in a fancy weave is superb for a pillow in a bedroom, a bathroom, or a beach house where fading might be a problem.

SATEEN

More informal than silk satin, cotton sateen comes in a range of colors, so it can be used as pillow backing, as piping, or as a frame for a special piece of embroidery.

TARTAN

Tartan is associated with Scottish clans though I've been told it originated in Spain as *tiritana*. Most often made of wool or worsted, tartans can also be made in many fibers and weights. Pillows of suitable tartan work well in a library or den. The fabric can be fringed to make an edging for the pillow, or it can be simply edged with a solid-colored piping.

TERRY

There are various weights of terry toweling (sometimes called terry cloth). Terry pillows are amusing on a terry-covered slipper chair in a bathroom or on a bathroom stool. If you cannot find terry cloth in a fabric store, use towels. I make pillows from facecloths by simply joining two together, incorporating the woven hems as decoration. Terry pillows can be embellished with lace, eyelet, or other trimmings, but keep them washable, and use washable polyester filler.

TICKING

Ticking has become a favorite for casual slipcovers and makes interesting, easygoing pillows if the stripes are cleverly mitered.

OTHER FABRICS

EMBROIDERY

There are myriad forms of embroidery and many of them work well on a pillow because of the relatively small area to be embellished. Embroidery can be quite elaborate—even dimensional—or delicate, because many pillows are purely decorative and not heavily used. Here are some examples of types of embroidery.

Appliqué

For this kind of embroidery, motifs are cut from fabric and applied to the base pillow fabric with any number of types of stitches, ranging from simple, turned-in hems to fancy herringbone stitches. Appliqués can be glued on, then stitched by machine. They can have embroidery, beads, or lace added to give dimension and details. If you study the seventeenth-century embroidery I made into a pillow on page 21, you will see that tiny lace collars and cuffs and beading have been applied to enliven the tiny embroidery stitches. Save small scraps of fabric that you can use to appliqué. Keep a file of design ideas for inspiration, such as folk art motifs (which are often simple), or if you do not trust your own originality, see what is available at your local craft store.

Crewelwork

Crewelwork is embroidery on linen using wool yarns called crewel. Transfers for crewel embroidery designs can be found in craft stores, or you can invent your own.

Cutwork

Cutwork is the name given to embroidery when shapes are cut out, then the edges are embroidered around.

Embroidering on the Home Machine

Whether or not you want to attempt to embroider by machine depends on the characteristics of your sewing machine and your own skill. Some machines make variations of zigzag stitches that can be embroidered in rows to produce striped effects.

Another method of machine embroidery that can give an interesting free-form effect is to take the foot off the machine, place your fabric in a large embroidery hoop, and move the hoop in any direction in order to "draw" with the machine needle. This way you can incorporate any color you wish onto your pillow.

Ethnic Embroidery

Into this category I put all those Far Eastern, Middle Eastern, and Native American hand embroideries that incorporate not only stitched threads, but also appliqué, beads, ribbon, shells, leather, padding, metallic thread, and mirrors. Antiques shops, thrift shops, and flea markets are the places to search for the real thing. To invent your own, keep a file of ideas for inspiration, a box of beads, and a box of exotic trimmings.

Eyelet

When hand-done, eyelet embroidery—also called *broderie anglais*—is made by pushing holes into the fabric with a stiletto rather than cutting them out. You can design and hand-embroider your own eyelet boudoir pillow in cotton or fine linen.

Fagoting

Fagoting is a simple form of *drawn-thread work,* or *hemstitching.* Drawn-thread work is often found on household linens. If you can find vintage linens, they can be recycled into effective pillows for a bedroom.

Household Linens

In the not-too-distant past of hope chests, household linens were embroidered with loving care. I was lucky in that my mother had two great-aunts who were excellent needlewomen but never married, and I inherited much of their work, including tray cloths, tea table cloths, pillow slips, doilies, handkerchiefs, and embroidered runners. I find they are a continual source of embroidered fabric for making white-on-white bedroom pillows. For those without a cache of this sort, treasures can be found in antiques shops that specialize in vintage household linens. If the linens are stained in places, you can usually figure out an ingenious way to remove or cover the bad spot.

Lace

This is a large category of both fabric and trimming, encompassing many different techniques, some including embroidery. Some lace is used just for trimming, and comes in various widths. Others are wide piece goods. Their names often reflect their place of origin, where they would have been handmade. Nowadays most lace is made by machine in imitation of the original handmade lace. Antique handmade lace is superior, with its human imperfections being part of the charm. (See "Glossary of Terms" for some well-known types of lace.) Lace is especially useful for feminine boudoir pillows, both as trimming or for the body of a pillow. White or ecru lace can be laid over solid fabric of another color to tie the pillow in with the color scheme of the room. Vintage lace–covered pillows are very much sought after and can be seen in profusion on the most ladylike beds. (See the top-right photograph on page 21.)

Needlepoint

Probably the most popular form of embroidery for pillows, needlepoint has been with us for several centuries, and will probably be around for several more. Design kits are available for needlepointers who are not ready to invent their own patterns.

For many decorators, the most attractive needlepoint was done in the nineteenth century. If you can find Victorian needlepoint—increasingly expensive and getting rarer—it can be made up into probably the most desirable pillows of all. Some of the most exquisite pieces of antique needlepoint are worked with tiny beads. Stitches include *bargello, flame stitch, gros point,* and *petit point.* Needlepoint was used to decorate many things, from cushions to carpets, slippers to bellpulls. (For ways to convert a needlepoint bellpull into a pillow, see pages 68–69.) No matter how small the scrap, it can be mounted, framed, and made into a tiny pillow. Filled with bran, it can be used as a pincushion.

Patchwork

Plain squares of patchwork, such as patchwork madras (see Madras, page 17) are most easily made by machine. Complex patchwork has to be made by hand.

Quilting

To quilt the amount of fabric to make a pillow is easy. Quilting is often done now by machine, using a special chain stitch.

Left: Pillow forms come in many shapes and sizes, and can also be made at home. They can be filled with down, kapok, polyester fiberfill, or foam rubber. In one round basket is goose down, and in the other are gleanings from the clothes dryer, which come in handy for stuffing into corners.

Below: A selection of trimmings here include black and red rope on cord, red fan-edged and white fan-edged fringe, white cotton tassel fringe, blue and white corded gimp, blue wool moss fringe, doubled red silk moss fringe, brown and white cord on tape, red silk cord, and five varieties of fan-edged fringe.

Above left: A pillow made from real seventeenth-century embroidery depicts Susannah and the Elders. Scraps of real lace were used for collars and cuffs, and beads for eyes. Framing the embroidery is partly worn cord saved from another scrap next to a flat beige tape, all set onto peacock blue ottoman to give the rather muted colors a lift. At the edge is an antiqued metallic fringe.

Above right: A selection of lace and embroideries includes vintage household linens, machine- and handmade eyelet, crochet, lace on net, tatting, guipure, quilting, and cutwork.

Left: Antique and modern needlepoint pillows mingle on this velvet daybed. Two contemporary pillows were made by fashion designer Meredith Gladstone to commemorate the birth of our two daughters, Emma and Jassy, and the tartan-effect pillow was made by London antiques dealer Stephen Long as a present for Keith.

Antique folk-art patchwork quilts made in the United States, especially the bold and simple quilts made by the Amish, are quite different in character from those made in Europe. Many quilts used a combination of patchwork, appliqué, and other forms of embroidery. Being good at the needle crafts was a virtue in the nineteenth century, and as there were no patterns available, each craftsperson had to design her own schemes. This led to great creativity, which can be an inspiration to us all.

Many vintage quilts have survived from the early part of the twentieth century. Some exquisite quilts are all white. If there are badly worn parts which make the quilt unusable as a whole, enough can be rescued to make attractive pillows.

Surface Stitching

Wonderful pillows can be hand-embroidered in many different simple surface stitches. Some well-known stitches are *backstitch, blanket* stitch, *buttonhole* stitch, *chain* stitch, *cross*-stitch, *feather* stitch, *French knots, herringbone* stitch, *lazy daisy* stitch, *satin* stitch, and *stem* stitch.

When I was little, most girls learned these embroidery stitches in school. However, my daughter Jassy—who never had a formal lesson in embroidery—as a teenager worked out her own designs, used stitches of her own invention, and gave us embroidered pillows for Christmas.

Smocking

Smocking is a form of embroidery that can be adapted for use on a pillow to give a three-dimensional look. Smocking is done by gathering fabric into rows of tiny, very accurate folds, and embroidering on the top of the gathers. Smocking is often found on the sort of children's dresses that grandmothers buy, and also on lampshades.

Stump Work or Berlin Work

Stump work is the name given to a padded, dimensional embroidery that has been done since Elizabethan times. Antique stump work is rare and costly. However, with imagination, modern versions make fascinating pillows.

Trapunto

Trapunto is a form of linear quilting, originally embroidered by hand but now often imitated by machine. For something as small as a pillow, hand work is more controllable and more eye-catching.

ATTIC SCRAPS

If you are like me, you accumulate bits and pieces "for a rainy day." Sometimes they are given to me by friends who hope I'll think of some way to use them. One such gift was a commemorative program of *Romeo and Juliet,* dated before the turn of the century and printed in pale gray and taupe lettering on silk satin. It made a thought-provoking pillow, bound with a piping of gray satin and backed with mouse-colored velvet.

Some scraps came from my family, such as a printed cotton handkerchief going back to when my grandfather fought in the Boer War. It was made into a pillow for a guest room. Small, unusual flags can be transformed into pillows. My husband Keith's grandmother—rather dreadfully—cut up her husband's embroidered Freemason's apron and stoles to make into pillows! She merely thought they were pretty, and had no idea they had spiritual significance. Keith has made pillows for a client out of her old Dior dress. Whether it be a piece of embroidered Chinese silk or an Indian gold-thread–embellished cloth, never discard precious remnants. Attic scraps have history and a warm, used quality that is impossible to duplicate with new fabric. Part of the challenge is how to make the scrap look its best. Right now I am debating what to do with a precious half yard of ribbon commemorating the wedding of Napoleon III to Eugénie de Montijo.

FELT

Felt comes in several weights and combinations—wool, fur, mohair, and some felts contain cotton or synthetics—and in a range of colors. It is useful in pillow making as a flange or edging for fur pillows, in much the same way that felt is used to outline a fur rug. The edges of felt can be pinked to give a nice finish. Felt is also useful as an appliqué fabric because it never needs to be finished off with a hem. The checkerboard pillow shown on page 59 is backed with dark green felt.

FUR

Fur may be our next endangered material. Save any scraps and worn-out or politically incorrect fur coats and use them for pillows. Fur is too beautiful to be discarded. Small pieces of fur can be mounted on fabric or leather to make a good-sized pillow. The flatter-piled furs are the easiest to handle, such as leopard, ocelot, and pony. I once made a pillow out of a discarded scrap of zebra with the mane running down the middle. (See the Framed Fur Pillow on page 75.)

HANDWOVEN TEXTILES

Contemporary craftspeople make interesting pillows for modern settings from fabric woven on hand looms. Yarns can be combined to produce unusual textures. I have seen a hand-woven textile incorporating tiny silver rings on a high-pile shaggy wool base and another that combined wool with fine leather strips. A pillow is an ideal size for this type of experimental weaving.

LEATHER

Leather can make handsome pillows for a library, den, or study. Leather comes in skins, with cowhide being the largest. Cowhides can have a smooth finish or can be brushed to resemble suede. Real suede is finer and comes in much smaller skins. Leather and suede can be dyed different colors, and also stamped, printed, or textured in various ways. Leather is also useful as a trimming. It can be made into piping or cut into strips—both plain or scalloped and punched to sew on without hemming. Leather can be cut into handsome fringes to go on fur or leather pillows.

RUGS

Good-looking pillows for masculine rooms can be made of scraps from worn-out antique rugs. Some of these textiles are very heavy and cannot be stitched on a regular sewing machine, especially if they are to be embellished with heavy cord, fringe, or tassels. You may have to sew them by hand, using carpet needles.

TRIMMINGS

BEADS

Beads have been used to embellish embroidery for centuries. Tiny bugle beads were used as accents such as eyes on the seventeenth-century embroidery I made into the pillow shown on page 21.

Victorian needlepoint was often picked out in little glass beads. Contemporary pillows can be given a three-dimensional quality with beads. Interior designer Mariette Himes Gomez told me about a beautiful pearl-embroidered pillow she made for a client.

There are many varieties of beads to be found in craft stores, including tiny ones you can use to restore beaded needlepoint, imitation pearls, shells, and wooden beads. Into this category I would also include spangles: sequins, which are sewn on flat through a center hole, and paillettes, which are larger and sewn on through a hole to one side so they can dangle. These can add glamour and sparkle to a pillow. Keep a box for your old or broken pieces of jewelry; they may come in very handy for a beaded pillow.

BUTTONS

Great-looking pillows can be made by using solid cloth—black, white, or colored—and sewing pearl buttons on in patterns (like a Cockney Pearly King's outfit) or just haphazardly. Keep a button bag, and never throw away a good button.

BRAID

Braid is a general term for a decorative trimming made from various fibers that is usually narrow but can be found up to 3 or 4 inches (8 or 10 cm) in width. Braid can be woven, tubular, or plaited.

CORD

The word *cord* can refer to several different items. Cable cord is a white cotton or polyester rope used in many ways, covered or uncovered. Piping cord is used as filler for piping or welting. Cord is also a form of heavy string used on window shades. Cords can be tubular decorative braids that can be hand-sewn onto pillows, around the edges, and into fancy curls. Decorative cord can also be bought attached to tape to be inserted into a seam before it is sewn.

FRINGE

Fringes are loose strands of yarn held on a heading. They can be made in any fiber, and come in many varieties. Here are a few that have more detailed descriptions in the Glossary of Terms: *beaded* fringe; *moss* fringe, sometimes called *brush* fringe; *rattail* fringe, also called *swag* fringe. There is also *block* fringe, *bullion* fringe, *fan-edged* fringe, *knotted* fringe, and *tassel* fringe. If the fabric you are using is suitable, you can pull threads out to make your own fringe—*self*-fringe—any length you choose, even doubled or tripled.

GIMP

Gimp is a woven trimming that comes in a variety of raised patterns. Although often used on wood-framed furniture to cover upholstery tacks and in many decorative ways on walls or the edges of lamp shades, it is also useful in pillow making as a braid to frame needlepoint or cover seams.

MACARON

Macaron is a French term used in the passementerie trade for a flat, buttonlike decorative motif usually covered in silk thread. It can be useful to embellish the corners or center of a pillow.

METALLIC

Fringes and braids can be found made of metallic, or metallic-looking yarns. Some of these have a dulled, antique look that works well with antique textiles. I have also found somewhat tarnished braid on old furnishings or clothing and recycled it successfully on pillows.

PIPING

Also called welting, piping is a filler cord covered with bias fabric. The way to make it is described in Chapter 3, "The Basic Pillow." Piping can be plain, gathered or ruched, or doubled.

RIBBON

Ribbon can be found in many colors, fibers, and sizes. Standard sizes are usually referred to by number, with ¼ inch (7 mm) being #1 and 3 inch (8 cm) being #40. Ribbon is used in pillow making as trimming in the form of a frame on the front surface, mitering the corners; trapped into the edge as a ruffle (in which case the ribbon should be wide enough to have a seam allowance); formed into a rosette; or actually woven into the pillow (see the Checkerboard Pillow on page 59.) Ribbon types include the following.

Grosgrain

Probably the most useful ribbon, grosgrain comes in many colors and sizes. To introduce more than one color and make your own striped ribbon, lay two or three different widths of grosgrain ribbon one on the other and topstitch them together.

Moiré

Moiré ribbon has a watered effect and can be found in a limited number of colors and sizes.

Picot-edged

This ribbon is silk, satin, taffeta, grosgrain, or velvet with a distinctive look due to its selvedges being embellished by tiny loops.

Satin

Especially useful for slotting through eyelet beading on a boudoir pillow, satin ribbon can be made of silk or of polyester, which is washable. The double-faced variety is best if you need to tie bows.

Patterned

Found in many colors, sizes, fibers, weaves, and prints, patterned ribbons range from narrow, simple stripes to wide tartan taffeta, and everything in between. In New York City, the ribbon stores that supply the garment district are around Thirty-eighth Street, between Fifth Avenue and Broadway. The ribbons you will find in these stores will make your mouth water, and most of the stores sell retail.

Velvet

Velvet ribbon is available in many colors, fibers, and sizes.

Antique

These interesting old ribbons are worth keeping an eye out for. Keith recently found some beautiful eighteenth-century narrow apple green ribbon embellished with pale pink shells forming flowers. It needed some steaming to gussy it up and then I used it on a pillow for a friend—someone I made sure would appreciate the ribbon's age and beauty—to frame an embroidered message.

RICKRACK

This inexpensive flat zigzag braid that can be bought in several sizes and colors at sewing stores should be used with caution as it tends to look like "loving-hands-at-home."

ROPE

Wide twisted cord is called rope. It can embellish pillows by being sewn by hand, along the edges, looped at the corners, or wound into spirals to decorate corners, or to outline the edge of needlepoint. Rope can also be bought attached to tape for insertion. Often the tape is natural colored even if the rope itself is dark in tone. If the rope on tape is thick, you may have to machine-stitch several times to get close enough to the rope to disguise the light-colored tape.

ROSETTE

A decorative motif similar to a macaron but with a softer, more dressmaker look, rosettes can be used to accent corners or the center of a pillow.

SOUTACHE

This is a narrow braid, originally used on military uniforms. It is usually topstitched in a central groove. Soutache can be used in a single row but is also effective used in several rows. It is narrow enough to turn corners without mitering.

TASSELS

There are many kinds of tassels, made from various materials. Elaborate tassels are formed on shaped wooden parts—head, body, skirt—and each part may be fancifully decorated. Simple tassels may be made by tying yarn into loops, wrapping yarn around the "head," and cutting the ends evenly. Tassels can be set in the gathers of French corners or right in the center of a pillow.

STUFFINGS

Much of a pillow's quality and feel depends on what goes into it. What you use for stuffing depends on the end use of the pillow. If it is to be luxuriously soft, such as a silk taffeta pillow, it should be stuffed

Above: An example of yo-yo patchwork made into a pillow can be seen in this upholstered chair.

Above: This selection of leather and fur includes, from left to right, red brushed cowhide, tan leather, a discarded leopard coat, brown brushed cowhide, a swatch book of leathers, some fake furs, and real zebra.

Right: My daughter Jassy embroidered this pillow and gave it to her sister, Emma, for Christmas to go on her bed. On the back she embroidered the moon and stars in silver and gold and the phrase "The sandman brings sleep." Jassy, a teenager then, had received no formal embroidery lessons. Being fiercely independent, she made up her own design and techniques.

Above: Displayed here is a selection of accumulated antique scraps and fabrics to be made into pillows. Starting at the top right corner: a pillow made from a satin banner commemorating a Royal Command performance of *Romeo and Juliet;* an 1853 ribbon commemorating the wedding of Napoleon III to Eugénie de Montijo; a red and gold Regency Greek key fabric cut into bands; a red and gold woven imberline; a nineteenth-century chintz; a red beaded, needlepointed bellpull; an antique metallic braid and a modern but antiqued gold fringe; a piece of yellow antique silk damask; Chinese silk embroidery on a blue ground; silk and gold brocaded fabric (foreground); a Victorian needle-point intended for a slipper; Victorian gros point (bottom right); flowers in petit point on ribbon; scraps of Victorian needlepoint to be made into tiny pillows; a vintage petit point and metallic embroidery intended for a purse (center); and an Indian white satin cloth embroidered in metallic threads.

with down, which is light and puffs up when plumped, filling the pillow better than any other stuffing. There are many blends of down and feathers. Make sure if there is a high percentage of feathers that they won't poke through your fabric and feel scratchy. Some people are allergic to down, but fortunately it is possible nowadays to use good-quality, soft-feeling man-made stuffings that are reasonably soft and resilient. Outdoor pillows must be washable, so some form of polyester is best for these. If a pillow is to be made from a rug or piece of tapestry, it should be firm, and kapok would be the right stuffing.

DOWNS AND FEATHERS

Eiderdown

This down, which comes from the eider, a northern seabird whose female uses the fine down to line her nest, has over the years given its name to the softest comforters. Though it is the best that can be had, nowadays it is too rare and costly for general use.

Goose Down and Goose Feathers

The best pillows and cushions are stuffed with goose down, which is expensive but luxurious. Goose down is lightweight, responds to the touch, and puffs up, filling with air when plumped. A less-costly filling is a mixture of goose down and goose feathers in varying proportions.

Chicken Down and Chicken Feathers

Chicken down is adequate for most cushions. Blends of down that have a core of chicken down surrounded with goose down will give a superior effect to pillows. A blend of chicken down and feathers can also be used, but the feathers tend to feel scratchy unless the fabric covering is dense or heavy.

KAPOK

Kapok is formed by a mass of silky fibers taken from the ceiba tree, which grows in tropical cli-mates. It is used for stuffing inexpensive pillows as well as mattresses, but it is heavy compared to down (and even to fiberfill), and tends to turn lumpy and limp with use. It is useful, however, in seat pads or pillows made from rug remnants, where firmness is more necessary than puffiness.

SYNTHETIC STUFFINGS

100% Polyester Fiber

Sometimes called fiberfill, this inexpensive synthetic fiber is popular and clean to use. It comes in pre-formed pillow shapes (large, small, square, oblong), loose in bags, or in sheets (called batting and useful for seat pads). Fiberfill has a somewhat fake, unyielding touch, but is useful to have on hand in its loose form to push into the corners of a pillow to smooth out wrinkles—the small amount needed for this won't affect the quality of the pillow. (If you do not have fiberfill at hand, a good trick is to save the lint from the drying machine and use that to stuff into the corners of a pillow. Lint has been washed and dried and will be fine in the small amounts you will need.)

Use fiberfill for the stuffing of a pillow if someone is allergic to feathers. Fiberfill also makes sense for pillows in a child's room—although feather pillows are what pillow fights are all about, they're no fun to clear up.

Foam

Foam is adequate for seat pads, especially for outdoor ones, but it is unsatisfactory for elegant pillows. Because foam tends to dry out and disintegrate after a time, it may result in pillows seemingly filled with powdery sand. Don't waste your time with foam unless it will be used for a long window seat, a bench, a seat pad that needs some height, or a banquette.

WHERE TO FIND STUFFINGS

Some companies that sell pillow interiors are listed in "Sources and Suppliers" at the end of the book. You can find suppliers under "Upholsterers' Supplies" in the Yellow Pages of the telephone book. Some companies will make up pillow interiors to individual specifications. This is worthwhile if you have to make a lot of pillows or if you need unusual shapes. Upholsterers' supply companies sell mainly to the trade at wholesale prices, but many are willing to also sell to retail customers.

Foam suppliers will often cut pieces to specifications. However, if you have to cut your own foam, it's easy to do with a sharp kitchen knife or an electric knife.

If there are no pillow or upholstery stores near you, you may have to buy regular bed pillows from a bedding or department store, selecting whichever blend of down or fiberfill that feels best. Choose a pillow shape as close as possible to the one you plan to make. If you need to alter the shape to suit your design and the pillow is not too tightly packed, shake the down to one side, tuck the excess fabric in to form a square pillow, and either topstitch the new shape by machine or sew by hand.

If the pillow bears no resemblance to your need in size or shape, very carefully and calmly transfer the feathers from the bought pillow casing to your own undercasing. Avoid wearing dark, fluffy clothes when doing this because feathers cling to everything.

PILLOW TICKING

Real ticking is very tightly woven cotton, usually with a distinctive railroad stripe in blue, red, or brown. The cloth, designed to cover pillows and mattresses, is constructed so that the sharp spines of feathers cannot penetrate the weave. It is the ideal fabric for a pillow casing form, but nowadays it is not always easy to find; most of the fabrics called "ticking" are ticking in looks only. As an alternative, use a tightly woven cotton fabric, such as high-thread-count cambric. Use double thickness if in doubt because feathers can insinuate themselves through most fabrics unless they are labeled downproof.

CHAPTER 3

THE BASIC PILLOW

The simplest pillow to make is a plain square, stitched around the edge, turned inside out, and filled with stuffing. Unadorned, knife-edged pillows—with simple seamed edges that have no piping trapped into them—can be wonderful, and all you may need if you select a beautiful fabric, such as pure silk taffeta, shantung, or damask in a glorious, singing color. Large 24-inch square, down-filled, plain silk pillows look magnificent at either end of a living room sofa, and are a good foil for smaller but more complex pillows placed next to them.

However, even to make a pillow as rudimentary as this requires refinement. If you were to cut an exact square, by the time you had stitched, turned, and stuffed it, instead of being a softened, inviting shape, the corners would poke out like rabbits' ears. As you will see in the instructions that follow, the right-angled corners of a square or rectangular pillow have to be trimmed off before stitching.

Most pillows require some decorative edging to fence them in with professional-looking fine detailing. This trimming can also introduce a color that will pull the room together as a whole. Even if a room is furnished in neutral colors, the pillows on upholstered furniture can add a shot of color that

will enhance the overall scheme. This can be accomplished by making pillows of an interestingly patterned fabric, such as a printed linen or chintz. The trimming can be a piping (often called welting) of solid fabric, the color chosen from the print, which might also be used elsewhere in the room (such as banding down the leading edges of the curtains, curtain lining, or even solid-colored pillows). Self-colored piping, too, adds definition and authority to a pillow; if the piping is gathered, the edging adds an interesting texture. Gathered piping can be subtle and narrow, only $\frac{1}{4}$ inch (7 mm) wide, or it can be fat, 1 inch (3 cm) in diameter, which gives the pillow a whole different look.

The following instructions will tell you how to decide the size and shape of a basic piped pillow; place the pattern accurately on a printed fabric; trim off the corners; cut and join bias strips for piping; make piping using a zipper foot; attach piping and assemble the pillow; turn, stuff, and sew up the seam; and finally, plump up the pillow to show it at its best.

Instructions will be given on inserting zippers and on making sham backs so that the pillow cover can be removed for cleaning or laundering. The added subtlety of ruched (also called shirred or gathered) piping will be described.

The four pillows on this sofa in a hall library are, clockwise from upper left, a red velvet zebra-painted pillow with a piped edge, a beaded needlepoint pillow with a corded edge, a knife-edged pillow in a provincial print with a piped edge, and a seaweed design–printed pillow with French corners.

BASIC PILLOW WITH SIMPLE PIPED EDGE

MATERIALS

Basic sewing equipment (see Chapter 1), including
    a zipper foot
Pillow form: a 20-inch (51-cm) form (see the top-left pho-
    tograph on page 20 and Stuffings, pages 25–29)
Piping filler cord: 2¼ yards (2.1 m) (see page 109)
Pillow fabric: ¾ yard (69 cm) to 1 yard (1 m) for front and
    back depending on the design repeat (see Diagrams 1,
    2, and 3 for design layouts)
Piping fabric, if it is to be of contrasting fabric: ½ yard
    (46 cm)
Matching thread

The amount of fabric needed for a basic 20-inch (51-cm) square pillow will depend on the placement and repeat of the print. As a general rule, 1 yard (1 m) of 45- to 50-inch-wide goods (1.28-m-wide) is enough for an average 20-inch (51-cm) square pillow; 1¼ yards if the pillow is to have self piping.

If the piping is to be cut from the same cloth as the pillow, it is known as self-piping, for which you should allow at least a ¼ yard extra fabric. If the piping is to be made from contrasting fabric, ½ yard (46 cm) should be sufficient. Piping is cut on the bias—at a 45-degree angle to the selvedge—which takes up quite a lot of cloth. Many stores will not sell less than ½ yard (46 cm) of fabric so you may not be able to buy just a ¼ yard. If the body of the pillow is a printed design, match the solid piping to a color in the print.

Many pillows are made with a print front and a contrasting solid fabric on the back. This can be the same solid colored fabric used for the piping or it can be yet another color selected from the print on the pillow front. Three-quarters of a yard (69 cm) will be sufficient for the back.

METHOD

Step 1: Once the fabric is selected and the pillow size chosen, establish where to place the print design on the pillow front. Marking and cutting correctly often takes time but makes the subsequent sewing much simpler. Cutting fabric that has a printed pattern requires "centering" the best part of the design on the pillow. Though there are many other print variations, Diagrams 1, 2, and 3 indicate different ways of placing the design you have selected for the front of the pillow on different fabric layouts when cutting. As shown by Diagram 3, a

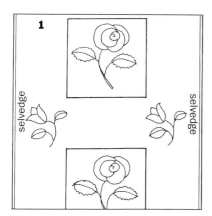

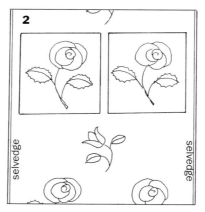

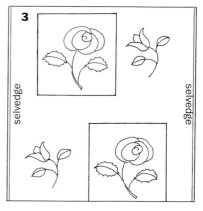

1. The most important design element in this fabric layout is in the center of the goods. If the back and front of the pillow are to be identical, this can be a wasteful way to cut because although it makes an attractive pillow from both sides, the edges of the fabric are not used.

2. On this layout the major design elements are side by side on the fabric, making it the least wasteful way to cut a pillow with identical front and back.

3. This layout shows the major design to be repeated on the diagonal. It is more wasteful to cut than the previous

layout if the front and back of the pillow are to be identical. However, if the secondary, less-pronounced part of the design is attractive, this can be centered on the back of the pillow, a layout that will require half the amount of fabric.

different (but centered) part of the print can be used on the back of the pillow.

A pillow tends to squash down with use, so center the design 1 inch (3 cm) above the true middle if it is a one-way pattern—that is, if the pillow will never be displayed on its side or upside down.

STEP 2: For the average 20-inch (51-cm) pillow, use a right-angled ruler to mark a true square the size of the pillow form on the wrong side of the fabric. If the pillow is firm, allow ½-inch (13-mm) seams, which will make the pillow fit the form snugly. If it is loosely stuffed, cut a 20-inch, or even a 19-inch square, and the pillow will end up smaller but firm. If you cannot see the design clearly from the wrong side, mark the square with pins or, *very lightly,* with pencil or tailor's chalk on the right side, once you have allowed ½-inch (13-mm) seam allowance (see Diagram 4).

Note: You may decide to use a premade cording with a tape attached for insertion instead of self-made piping, or else a premade piping. If so, allow the same amount of seam allowance on the pillow as on the tape insertion, which will make the job easier to sew. The tapes that are attached to cording may be anything from ⅜ inch to ¾ inch (1 cm to 2 cm) wide.

If you are using a striped or checkered fabric, be sure the patterns are centered and that the front and back match at the edges.

STEP 3: Cut 2 pieces, a front and a back; they can be different fabrics. Cut a notch at the center bottom of both the front and the back (see Diagram 5). Follow the directions in Diagram 6 to shape the pieces so the corners do not stick out.

STEP 4: Make the piping following the instructions in Diagrams 7 through 11. Self-piping is cut from the same fabric as the body of the pillow.

Piping, sometimes called welting or cording, is filler cord covered with fabric. The fabric for piping must be cut on the bias so it has enough flexibility to turn corners without wrinkling.

Note: For large amounts of piping, for a sofa for instance, bias can be cut in one continuous strip. This is not usually necessary for one or two pillows.

Piping or filler cords vary in diameter from ⅛ inch (3 mm) to 1 inch (3 cm) and can be found in good upholstery and fabric stores. To determine the width of bias needed to cover the filler cord, place a cloth tape measure or a piece of fabric over the filler and add ½-inch (13 mm) seams. Add ¾-inch (2 cm) seams for any filler cord more than ¾ inch (2 cm) in

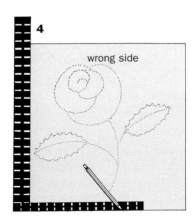

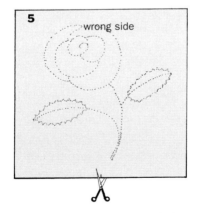

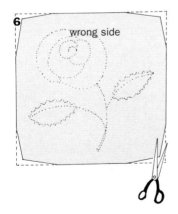

4. Using a right-angled ruler, mark the fabric on the wrong side of the cloth with pencil or tailor's chalk, allowing a ½-inch (13-mm) seam allowance.
5. Cut a notch at the center bottom of both the front and the back pieces of fabric. This is especially important if the

fabric has a nap or a one-way design.
6. To keep the pillow corners from sticking out in points—which happens if you cut a perfect square—mark in from each corner 0 inch (00 cm) on a 20-inch (51-cm) pillow. Draw a line from this point to one-quarter the length of the

pillow edge at each corner. Cut along this line. On a 22-inch (56-cm) pillow, measure ¾ inch (2 cm) in from each corner; on a 24-inch (61-cm) pillow, measure in 1 inch (3 cm).

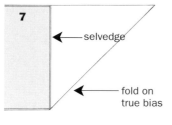

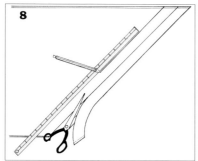

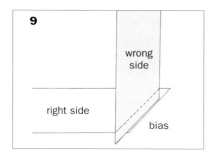

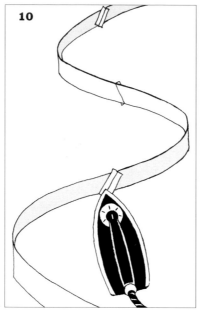

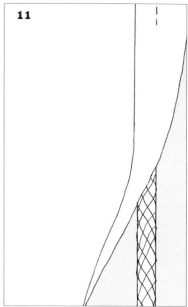

7. The true bias is at a 45-degree angle to the selvedge. Establish the bias by folding the crosswise grain along the selvedge.

8. Using a pencil or tailor's chalk, mark 1½-inch (4-cm) strips on the bias. For the small amount needed for a pillow, cut separate bias strips.

9. To join the strips into a continuous piece, place the right sides of the fabric facing each other with the two strips at right angles, aligning them to allow a ¼-inch (7-mm) seam allowance. Machine-stitch each seam and trim the threads. Repeat seaming until all the bias needed is in one continuous length.

10. Press the seams open and trim off the protruding seam allowances.

11. With the wrong side of the strip (showing the seam allowances) facing upward, lay the piping cord lengthwise in the center and wrap the bias strip over the cord, keeping the raw edges together evenly. Thread the sewing machine with matching thread and put on the zipper foot. With the zipper foot to the right of the machine needle, stitch close to the raised swelling made by the cord, trapping the cord in the bias strip of fabric snugly but not squashing it or stitching on top of it.

diameter. When you flatten out the tape measure or the fabric, you will have the width needed for piping. Standard ¼-inch (7-mm) piping generally requires strips 1½ inches (4 cm) wide.

To establish the length of bias needed for one pillow, measure along one edge of the pillow form and multiply by four.

Attach the piping to the pillow front as shown in Diagrams 12 through 17.

STEP 5: When the piping has been made and applied to the front of the pillow, lay the back of the pillow to the front, right sides facing in, and match up the center bottom notches. Using the previous stitching as a guide but stitching closer to the piping, sew the two together, leaving a space of about 14 inches (35 cm) either along the bottom or at the side. As a general rule, the opening is better at the side, because it is best to make a firm machine stitch at the center bottom where the piping or cording have been joined. It will also be easier to stitch up the seam where the piping or cording is all in one piece.

STEP 6: Follow instructions in Diagrams 18 through 20 to complete the pillow.

STEP 7: When the pillow is completed, dress it down by plumping it in every direction so that the

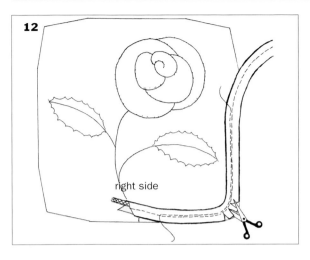

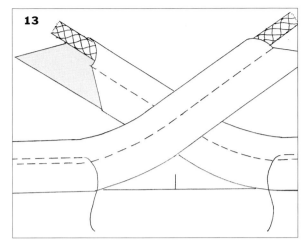

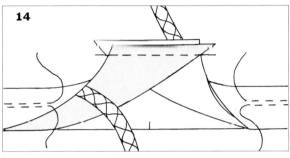

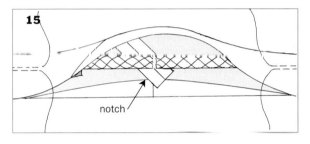

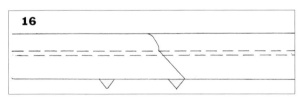

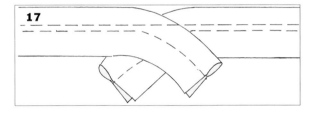

12. Apply the piping to the front of the pillow first. With the front right side up, lay or pin the piping so that ¼ inch (7 mm) of piping goes to the other side of the center bottom notch. Matching the raw edge of the pillow with the raw edges of the piping, allow 3 inches (8 cm) beyond that point before machine-stitching with the zipper foot. Take just under a ½-inch (13-mm) seam, using the stitching on the piping as a guide and going just a hair beyond them. This ensures that the stitches on the piping will be completely hidden on the finished pillow. At the corners, cut several notches for a rounded effect. (For a more pronounced corner, cut a single notch.)

13. The best method for joining the ends of the bias piping is to stop stitching about 2 inches (5 cm) before coming back all the way to the center bottom notch. Allow the piping ends to overlap at least 1 inch (3 cm) before cutting the piping off.

14. Rip open both ends of the piping, thus separating the bias fabric from the cord. Allow the piping fabric a ¼-inch (7-mm) seam allowance beyond the center bottom notch, then cut on the straight of the grain, matching the slanting ends of the fabric strips. Align the bias strips so that they form a seam that will appear to be a slanting seam on the wrong side. Pin them, and check before stitching the seam that the piping is the right length. Stitch, then press

open the seam with the back of your nail.

15. Overlap the raw cords and lay them flat against the bias fabric. Cut through both cords to make the ends butt exactly.

16. Lay the bias fabric over the cord and stitch. The slanting seam should now lie as smoothly as any other seam in the piping. Sew the encased piping to the pillow.

17. An alternative method for finishing off piping cord, simpler but less professional, is to overlap the piping at the center bottom of the pillow. To do this, pull the cord out from both ends of the piping at the point where they overlap and snip it away. Then overlap the piping and stitch it in place.

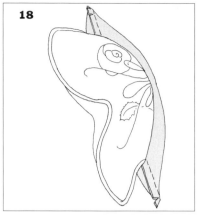

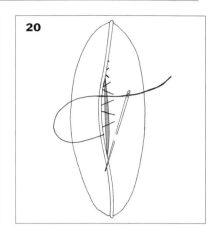

18. Turn the pillow right side out.
19. Stuff in the pillow form. If the corners seem a little empty, tuck in extra fiberfill stuffing or a small wad of clean fluff from the dryer.
20. Hand-sew the opening using what I

call a "ladder stitch," though it is sometimes called a blind stitch or slip stitch. Double thread or heavy upholstery thread is best. Sewing behind the piping, take even stitches from one side, then the other, pulling the thread gently

to draw the edges together evenly as you go. Keep checking to make sure the seam is smooth with no puckers on one side or the other when you get to the end of the opening.

down separates, expands with air, and fills each of the corners.

Once you have made a basic pillow, it is possible to master many other techniques of pillow making.

ZIPPERS

Although most pillows made of really elegant fabrics are better off ladder-stitched at the seam, some casual pillows that require frequent washing or cleaning may need zippers.

Zippers can be sewn along the bottom back of the pillow once the trimming, such as a simple piping, has been added. Select a zipper that is just an inch or two short of the width of the pillow. Use a zipper foot when setting in the zipper.

If the trimming is thick, or the piping or cord or tape is heavy, or the pillow has ruffles, but you still need a zipper opening, the zipper is best set into the back body of the pillow. To do this, when cutting the pillow back be sure to allow an extra $1\frac{1}{2}$ inches (4 cm) to be split into two $\frac{3}{4}$-inch (2-cm) zipper seams. Cut the seam low on the back of the pillow so it will be as invisible as possible, but bear

in mind that the pillow will not be reversible. Select a zipper the exact width of the pillow and set the zipper in, using the zipper foot, before assembling the rest of the pillow.

SHAMS

Some pillows, especially boudoir pillows for bedrooms and often-washed pillows for children's rooms, are best made rather like bed pillows with a "sham" back so that the interior can be very easily removed.

Shams are made by cutting the back of the pillow in two overlapping pieces. The opening can be in the middle of the back or to one side. On a square pillow it can be vertical or horizontal, but the opening holds better when it is vertical on a rectangular pillow. Diagram 1 on the facing page gives the instructions for making a sham.

Shams can also be charming when less deeply overlapped and buttoned. If you do not have a sewing machine that is able to make buttonholes, you can easily hand-embroider the few buttonholes needed. The instructions for a buttoned sham are given in Diagram 2, following.

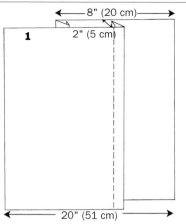

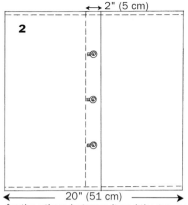

1. Whereas a zipper is usually set in horizontally, the sham opening is often vertical. For a 20-inch (51-cm) pillow, allow a 4-inch (10-cm) overlap, plus 2-inch (5-cm) turnbacks on either side, making each half of the pillow back 21 inches (53.5 cm) by 16½ inches (42 cm). Crease and press the turnbacks 2½ inches (6.5 cm) in, and turn in a ½-inch (13 mm) seam to hide the raw edge. Topstitch or hand-hem. Overlap the two back pieces and check that the back matches the front. Machine-stitch along the edges of the back so that it forms one single piece, then proceed as for a basic pillow.

2. For a buttoned sham allow a 1½-inch (4-cm) overlap and 2-inch (5-cm) turnbacks. Select 3 buttons (they can be self-covered). Mark for a horizontal buttonhole in the center of the overlap and for the others between it and the top and bottom. Check that the back and front match, then make machine or hand-sewn buttonholes. Machine-stitch around the edges to form a single back piece and continue as for the basic pillow.

GATHERED PIPING

To make a pillow with a gathered piping, you work the same way as for plain piping (see Step 4 on page 33). To add the proper fullness, you need three times the length of bias strips.

METHOD

STEP 1: As you make the piping, gently push the bias covering fabric with your fingers or the tips of closed scissors so that it forms gathers. When there is enough gathered piping for the pillow, adjust the gathers so they are evenly distributed, then topstitch to hold the gathers firmly.

STEP 2: Sew the gathered piping to the front of the pillow as you would plain piping (see Diagram 12).

STEP 3: Make a slanted seam in the piping, butt the piping filler, and topstitch over the gathered seam.

STEP 4: Sew the front and back of the pillow together, using the previously sewn stitches as a guide but stitching just a hairbreadth closer to the piping. Leave an opening for turning (see Step 5 on page 34.)

STEP 5: Turn the pillow right side out, stuff in the pillow form, and sew up the opening. Finally, dress down the pillow. (See Steps 6 and 7 on page 34.)

The pillows shown in the photograph on page 38 have extra-large gathered piping. You need filler cording at least ¾ inch (2 cm) to 1 inch (3 cm) in diameter. Filler this wide is usually made of fat cotton strands bound lightly with a mesh of finer cotton threads. Cut your bias strips as wide as needed, according to the previous instructions for making plain piping.

DOUBLE PIPING

Having mastered making a regular piping, it is a simple matter to make double piping. This is particularly useful if you wish to introduce two colors into the edging of a pillow but cannot find a ready-made multicolor cord.

Double piping can be two pipings of the same width, or one piping can be wider than the other—say an outer piping ¼ inch (7 mm) in diameter and an inner piping ⅛ inch (3 mm) in diameter. However, double pipings wider than ¼ inch (7 mm) in diameter are clumsy to sew.

Double piping is best made of fabric that is not

The pillows on the sofa in the living room of decorator Maryanne Oberlin in Hudson, Ohio, have extralarge gathered piping around their edges.

too bulky, as eventually six thicknesses of fabric will have to be stitched through. Plain glazed chintz is ideal because it can be found in many colors. If you prefer a matte effect, simply use the chintz on the wrong side. Cotton or silk taffeta is also available in a range of colors and is thin enough. If the actual pillow fabric you are using is cotton, it is better to use a cotton piping. Likewise, if you are using silk, use silky fabric for the piping.

A double piping can be used satisfactorily only on a pillow that has a front and a back because the back of the double piping shows a line of stitching. For this reason, it is suggested that double pipings be used on one-sided pillows (such as needlepoint

pillows, painted pillows, and pillows that are fancy on the front but plain on the back), or on ruffled pillows between the body of the pillow and the ruffle, so that the ruffle hides the back of the piping.

METHOD

STEP 1: Once the piping fabrics are chosen, decide which color should be on the outside of the double piping; for this color, cut the bias strips 1 inch (3 cm) wider than for the inner piping. Cut the same length of bias strips in both colors.

STEP 2: Join the bias strips and press the seams open. Using the zipper foot and your chosen piping filler, make up each color of piping. (See the instructions for piping in Step 4 on page 33.) The outer piping will have a larger seam allowance.

STEP 3: Lay the narrower piping alongside the wider one and stitch the two together as closely as possible using the zipper foot (as shown below).

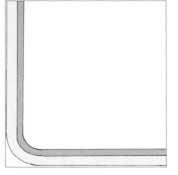

Detail of double welt on the edge of a pillow.

STEP 4: Apply the piping to the pillow front as for plain piping (see Diagram 12, page 35) and then join and finish the pillow as previously (see Steps 5 through 7 on pages 34–36).

Adapting these simple, basic techniques, you can produce any number of variations, creating versatile pillows that range from a simple square to complex piped pillows, depending on the overall need of your room.

SPECIAL TECHNIQUES
FOR PILLOWS

A knife-edged pillow with a piped edge like the one described in the previous chapter is so basic that almost anyone can make one. These simple pillows are ideal for fabric such as chintz where further embellishment is not only unnecessary but might also detract from the printed design. There are other techniques in pillow making that are more complicated but can be mastered easily, and involve no more special materials than those needed for a plain piped pillow. I will explain in this chapter special techniques for making French corners, ruffles, flanges, and much more.

For example, if you have your heart set on using a striped fabric, there are many ways you can cut and piece the fabric to make a unique pillow. I will offer some stripe ideas that may spark your imagination.

Or if the fabric you have selected needs something other than a matching or contrast piping, there are lots of ready-made trimmings to choose from, such as braids, cords, fringes, and tassels. Choosing the most appropriate one for your needs is important. Applying them may require different techniques, using both machine and hand sewing. Pillows with appropriate trimmings can make all the difference to a sitting room.

One very nice touch is to use ribbons, which are found in many handicraft stores. They can be used in various ways in pillow making. They can be inserted into the edges like a flange, or shirred like a ruffle. They can be sewn on flat, like a braid. They can even be woven into whole pillows. Depending on the ribbons, they can be ultrasweet for a baby's nursery, or tough enough to use in a game room, like one shown in the photograph on page 59.

Try to find old-fashioned household linens, which nowadays are seldom used for their original purposes. How many of us—except as a sort of throwback joke—use the delicate lace-edged doilies that would have enhanced the tea tables of Victorian and Edwardian ladies? How often do we use elaborately embroidered tray cloths on our guests' breakfast trays? Do our bureaus and dressing tables today have hand-stitched runners and mats? These precious vintage linens can be taken out of their lavender-scented drawers and recycled, with a little ingenuity, as delicious boudoir pillows. Ahead are lots of ideas for making lacy pillows that can dress up a bed, or be scattered on a chaise longue in a dressing room.

Make your bathrooms cozy and comfortable with a cushion or two on a bamboo, wicker, or upholstered slipper chair. Bathroom pillows can be made of vintage linen hand towels, in wonderful-quality bird's-eye weave, or honeycomb weaves, using the handmade crochet edges, embroidered bands, or knotted fringes found on these treasures from the past. And what fabric is more suitable for a pillow in a bathroom than terry toweling, made more individual with a frosting of lace or fringe?

Whether you use what you already own or have to start out with brand-new material, here are some more easy techniques that will help you to create your own special pillows.

FRENCH CORNERS

You may have noticed pillows that are square or rectangular but nevertheless have a rounded, plump look with soft gathers in each corner. These are generally called French corners, though they are sometimes described as Turkish corners, butterfly corners, or gathered corners. The pillow in the photograph on page 30 in red and pink seaweed-patterned chintz is an example of a pillow with French corners.

French corners are popular because they give a softened and more dimensional look to a pillow. They also appear slightly smaller than a basic knife-edged pillow because they are fatter. Bear this in mind when deciding what size to make.

Sometimes pillows with French corners have piping or cording in the seam around the edge. You may even find a silky tassel set in the gathers at each corner, making a cushion look ready for a Turkish potentate to recline on.

You should not use French corners on certain pillows, such as those made with framed needlepoint, or painted pillows, or any pillows where the soft gathers at the corners might distort the design of the central motif. French corners are difficult to make on pillows of heavy or rugged textiles such as kilims.

1. To make a French corner, mark a slant at each corner on the wrong side. On a pillow 20-inches (51-cm) square or larger, measure 4 inches (10 cm) from the corners. On smaller cushions mark 3 inches (8 cm) from the corners. Gather inside marked line, or cut along line if the pillow will have a piped edge.

2. To pleat French corners instead of gathering across the slanting corner, use the tips of your fingers to fold an inverted pleat, then fold pleats on either side. Stitch over the pleats by machine.

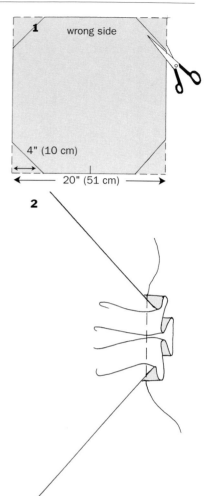

METHOD

STEP 1: Instead of slivering off the corners as you would for a basic pillow, mark the corner with chalk or pencil in a pronounced slanting angle. This slanting line is then pulled together in gathers or pleats. Diagram 24 shows how to mark the corners.

STEP 2: The slanted corner can be gathered by hand, with the full corner left on. Many beginners prefer to gather the corners by hand, using heavy thread or double thread along the marked line with the corner uncut. Another method is to sew with a zigzag stitch—if your machine can do this—over a piece of string along the marked line with the corner uncut, which can then be pulled up tight to form gathers. Machine-stitch several times over the

gathers with a regular stitch just avoiding the string, then pull the string out. If you aren't going to use piping, the gathering can be done after the front and back have been stitched together.

STEP 3: If piping or any kind of trim is to be used, do the gathering first on each corner, back and front separately, before the trim is added. I find it easier to cut the corner off completely so that there is an exact line to gather or pleat up. If you practice, you can gather on the machine by holding your finger or the points of your scissors close behind the machine needle to shirr up the material as you stitch.

I find that it is both quicker and more accurate to make tiny pleats instead of gathers; this can also be done on the sewing machine. See Diagram 2 at left. With your fingers, fold 2 pleats to meet in the center, then 2 more on either side. Press the pleats down firmly with your nail, then sew by machine over the 4 pleats.

STEP 4: Piping or cording on tape is then applied over the pleats or gathers, and the front and back of the pillow are joined together. The pillow is finished as usual.

RUFFLES

Ruffles are a well-established way to edge a pillow, though ultrafeminine ruffles come and go in popularity. Ruffles can be set into the edges of pillows, be made in all sizes, be of all one color or pattern matching the body of the pillow, or have one color on the front and another at the back. There are many possible variations (as shown by the diagrams below).

There are many reasons for adding ruffles to pillows. You may want to introduce large or small amounts of specific colors to a room to help pull it together visually. Ruffles can also provide a solid "fence" around a pillow of patterned fabric. And they make a pillow appear specially designed and custom-made.

APPLYING BINDING TO A RUFFLE

To introduce or emphasize color on a pillow, ruffles can be bound along the edge with a flat ¼-inch (7-mm) solid binding. Binding can be put on a single ruffle, or on the edges of double ruffles. The fabric you select for binding should be lightweight, such as a solid chintz to go on a cotton pillow, or a silk taffeta to go on a silk pillow. The binding must be applied before the ruffle is gathered and set into the pillow.

The two methods for applying binding on a ruffle are discussed on page 42.

1. Tiny ruffles no more than ⅜ inch (1 cm) wide can look suave on large, down-stuffed, French-cornered pillows.

2. Pillows can also be ultrafeminine, gussied-up, and elaborate with ruffles that are 3 or 4 inches (8 cm or 10 cm) wide.

3. Ruffles can be double or even triple of different widths and colors, but these are best made in lightweight fabrics for very feminine rooms.

4. A piping—or a double piping or a fringe—can be set between the body of the pillow and the ruffle to introduce specific colors into a room or to emphasize colors.

METHOD 1

This first method involves both machine stitching and hand stitching using single fabric for the binding.

STEP 1: Cut bias strips 1 inch (3 cm) wide. The amount should equal the length of the ruffle.

STEP 2: Join bias strips to make one continuous strip, pressing open the seams with an iron and snipping off the projecting seam corners.

STEP 3: Press in ¼-inch (7-mm) turnings at the top and bottom of the strip.

STEP 4: Press the binding over in half to form a bias binding ¼ inch (7 mm) wide.

STEP 5: Opening the binding, lay the raw edge of the binding against the right side of the edge to be bound. Stitch by machine in the first fold of the binding. See Diagram 1.

STEP 6: Turn the binding over to the wrong side. With tiny stitches, as invisible as possible, hem the binding (see Diagram 2).

As you will see, this is a time-consuming method, but its advantage is that the binding is lightweight because it is only a single thickness.

METHOD 2

The second method is used far more often commercially because it is quicker, uses double fabric, and can all be done by machine.

STEP 1: Cut bias strips 2¼ inches (6 cm) wide.

STEP 2: Seam and press open the seams as in Method 1.

STEP 3: Press in half lengthwise, forming a bias strip with a fold at one side.

STEP 4: Place the raw edges of the bias strip on the right-side edge of the ruffle to be bound. Sew it on taking a ¼-inch (7-mm) seam allowance (see Diagram 3).

STEP 5: Fold the double binding over to the wrong side and press it, then machine-stitch in the groove from the right side, catching the binding on the wrong side as you stitch, as shown in Diagram 4.

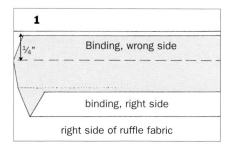

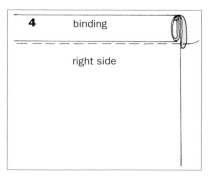

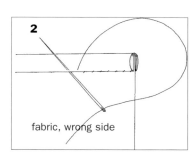

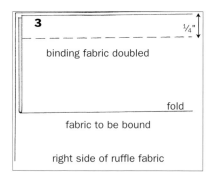

1. Sew the pressed single bias binding onto the edge of a ruffle.
2. Hand-hem the single binding on the wrong side.
3. Sew the double bias binding onto the right side of the ruffle.
4. Turn the binding over to the wrong side and press it so that ¼ inch (7 mm) shows on the right side. There should be ⅜ inch (1 cm) of binding with a clean-finished edge on the wrong side. From the right side, stitch by machine in the groove between the ruffle and the binding, catching ⅛ inch (3 mm) of the wrong side of the binding as you sew.

Double ruffles—such as these seen on pillows in the New York apartment of Mrs. Peter Gregory—can be the same width. Lining the inner sides of the ruffle with a contrasting fabric adds a subtle flash of color. The small pillows have lightly shirred ribbon edging.

PLEATED RUFFLES

You can use similar ruffle-making techniques for both pressed or unpressed pleated frills around pillows. When making pleats, cut the fabric to be pleated on the straight rather than on the bias, and fold on the double. For sharply pressed pleats, make even creases with the iron, then stitch the pleats in along the raw edges before attaching to the pillow. Unpressed pleats do not have to be pressed. However ⅜-inch (1-cm) unpressed pleats around a pillow give a more tailored effect than gathers.

RUFFLES WITH PIPING

Ruffles can also be set on a pillow with piping (see Diagram 4 on page 41). An example of this is a pillow made of eyelet embroidered fabric with an eyelet embroidered ruffle. It can be seen on page 51 along with instructions for making this pillow.

CUTTING RUFFLES

Unless you are going to use a decorative border along the selvedge as a ruffle, ruffles look softest and most elegant when they are cut on the bias, and therefore they take up a lot of yardage. Depending on the fabric used, ruffles may have to be as much as three times as long as the edge of your pillow in order to give luxurious fullness. This is called gathering 3 to 1 in cutting terms. Heavy, or very patterned fabrics are better gathered 2½ times to 1. Ruffles usually need to be cut double the finished width so that they can be pressed in half, making them clean-finished on both sides. Bear in mind, therefore, that ruffles take up more goods than the body of a pillow.

You will have to see some seams in the ruffles, so if you are using a patterned fabric, match these seams accurately. However, since the ruffles are on the bias, they do not have to match up to the body of the pillow at any point even if the ruffle is from the same fabric as the body of the pillow. Make sure you have the right width and length for the ruffles before cutting. Do not rush the cutting process. Cutting, especially matching on the bias, often takes longer than the stitching process, but if

you cut accurately the stitching is made easier.

Try out various ideas for ruffles before you make final decisions, because mistakes using decorative fabrics can be costly. To experiment, lay squares of fabrics folded to pillow size on your sofa. Cut small strips of contrasting fabric to simulate piping, ruffles, and bindings, and consider many possibilities before you cut.

PILLOW WITH RUFFLES

The simple 20-inch (51-cm) overall pillow described here has 2-inch (5-cm) ruffles made of the same fabric as the body of the pillow.

MATERIALS

Basic sewing equipment
Pillow interior: suitably sized
Pillow fabric: from 1½ yards (1.5 m) to 2 yards (2 m) depending on the design and width of the material. If the selected fabric has a specific design motif, decide where this design should be centered. You will be able to use both the front and the back of the pillow, so you may want to put the same design on the back. However, you may prefer to use another part of the design for the back. Before cutting, consider all of these possibilities. See Diagram 1 for a layout suggestion.

METHOD

STEP 1: Since the front is the most noticeable part of the pillow, mark it first. Mark a 17-inch (43-cm) square on your fabric. If the pattern is one-way, make the center point 1 inch (3 cm) higher to allow for pillow slouch. Mark on the wrong side of the fabric in case you change your mind. Mark also where you will shave off the corners (see Diagram 6, page 33).

STEP 2: Before actually cutting the fabric, find the true bias (see Diagram 7, page 34) and make sure you have room to cut the ruffles before marking and cutting the back of the pillow. You will need true bias strips 5 inches (13 cm) by 5 yards (4.6 m). You may have many seams, but they must match if the print design is very obvious. Mark the ruffles, then mark a 17-inch (43-cm) square for the back of the pillow.

STEP 3: Cut the front and back, trimming off the corners as you did for the basic pillow. You may find it easier to lay the cut front onto the fabric as a pattern when cutting the back. Notch the center bottom of both the front and the back.

STEP 4: Cut the strips for the ruffles and then pin the seams together to ensure that they match.

STEP 5: Sew the seams of the ruffles to form one long bias strip. Join the end to the beginning to form a continuous ring.

STEP 6: Press the seams open, checking that they all match. Press the ruffle in half lengthwise, making sure the raw edges meet exactly.

STEP 7: Using a long machine stitch, sew along the raw edges to hold them together before gathering.

STEP 8: Divide the bias ring in half, then in quarters. Mark each of these points with a notch and a pin set in across the stitch, as shown in Diagram 35. The pins will match up with the corners of the pillow. Once the bias is gathered, a pin is easier to find than a notch; however, if the pin falls out, the notch gives you a second chance to be accurate.

STEP 9: Using the largest stitch on the machine, gather along the edge of the ruffle, $\frac{1}{8}$ inch (3 mm) inside the first holding stitch. Use a gathering foot if you like. You may prefer to gather the ruffle as I do by using your fingers or the tips of closed scissors. If you are a beginner, gather by hand using double thread for strength, taking small running stitches. Pucker up the gathers.

STEP 10: Pin the gathered ruffle to the pillow, matching the pins to the corners of the pillow front. Allow extra fullness at each corner. Make sure the

gathering is well distributed, then pin it all around, placing the pins *across* the gathering stitches.

STEP 11: Machine-stitch slowly and carefully over the gathers and the pins without necessarily removing the pins until you are finished. If you are nervous about breaking a machine needle, baste the ruffle in place. As you get more experienced, you will find less need for pinning or basting. As you stitch, make sure the raw edges all meet. The frill will be facing in toward the center of the pillow (see Diagram 3). Take a $\frac{1}{2}$-inch (13-mm) seam, which will be $\frac{1}{8}$ inch (3 mm) beyond your gathering stitch.

STEP 12: Matching the center bottom notches, lay the front of the pillow, complete with ruffle, onto

1. A good way to lay the pieces out when cutting ruffles is to cut the front and the back of the pillow staggered on the yardage, which leaves a bias strip of fabric between them to use for ruffles.

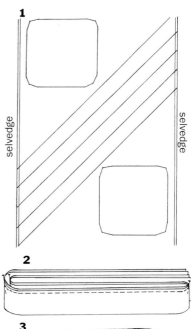

2. Divide the folded strip for ruffling into quarters and mark with notches and pins.

3. When stitching the front of a ruffled pillow to the back, push all the ruffles inward.

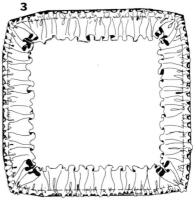

the pillow back and pin them together, with the ruffles lying inward between the front and the back. Using the previous stitch as a guide, sew front to back, leaving a 12-inch (30-cm) opening along one side for turning.

STEP 13: Turn the pillow inside out. Check to make sure you have not caught any gathers unevenly by mistake, which is easy to do. If so, snip open and restitch where needed.

STEP 14: Place stuffing into the pillow interior and smooth it carefully into the corners. Check to see if the pillow needs any extra stuffing in the corners, and if so, add some.

STEP 15: Ladder-stitch up the opening. Plump up the pillow and touch up the ruffle with an iron if necessary.

DOUBLE RUFFLES WITH CONTRASTING INNER SIDES

If you need to add just a flash of a contrasting color to a pillow, a subtle way to achieve this is to make double ruffles and line the insides of the ruffles facing each other with a contrasting solid fabric. For this kind of pillow, the fabric must be thin, such as chintz or taffeta. One yard (1 m) of contrasting fabric should be enough.

METHOD

STEP 1: Cut the body of the pillow as you did for the single-ruffle pillow (see Step 1 on page 44). The difference here is that you should cut the ruffles only 3 inches (8 cm) wide. The strip will be 10 yards (9 m) in length. Make sure the seams match if you are using a patterned fabric.

STEP 2: Cut the same amount, 3 inches (8 cm) by 10 yards (9 m), on the true bias in the contrast fabric.

STEP 3: Seam both the solid and the patterned bias strips into separate continuous strips. Make sure

both solid and patterned strips are the same length.

STEP 4: Cut each strip in half lengthwise (using a bias cut) to form 2 sets of ruffles. Join the ends of each strip to form 2 solid and 2 patterned rings.

STEP 5: Seam the patterned bias strips to the solid bias strips, taking a ¼-inch (7-mm) seam allowance to form 2 bias rings that are 5½ inches (14 cm) wide.

STEP 6: With an iron press, open the seams running through the middle of both rings, then fold the ruffle lengthwise and press the seams again. The fold that divides the solid from the patterned fabric must be knife sharp.

STEP 7: Sew a holding stitch on the raw edges of both rings of fabric, divide the rings into quarters, and mark with notches and pins as for the single-ruffle pillow (see Diagram 2, page 45).

STEP 8: Gather each ruffle separately. Matching the pins, stitch both ruffles together with the contrast fabric sides facing each other. Proceed as for the single-ruffle pillow (see Steps 10 through 15, pages 45–46).

FLANGED PILLOWS

A variation on the ruffle is the flange. Flanges look like ungathered ruffles—rather like ravioli. An example of a flanged pillow is shown in the photograph on the facing page.

Shapes on the edge of flanges can be straight, curved, scalloped, or pointed. They can be bound on the edge with a narrow binding (see Applying Binding to a Ruffle, page 41) or they can be clean-finished. They can be as narrow as 1 inch (3 cm) or as wide as 4 inches (10 cm). Generally flanges tend to be around 2 inches (5 cm) to 2½ inches (6.5 cm) wide. A flanged pillow can be cut all in one with its border, as shown in the diagram on page 48, which includes a border that is curved in a fanciful way.

This flanged pillow was inspired by antique Regency fabric woven in a Greek key design.

METHOD

STEP 1: Decide the shape you want and make a pattern out of paper. Fold the paper in half, to make the shape symmetrical, then draw the shape along half of one edge. On a fancy border like this, allow only ¼-inch (7-mm) seams so that the seam allowance will not be clumsy when it is turned in. Use this one edge to mark the four sides of the flange on the fabric.

STEP 2: Mark your pattern on the fabric and cut out the front and the back of pillow.

STEP 3: Put the right sides of the front and back together and stitch around the edge on the wrong side, leaving a space to turn. Notch around the curves and in the angles so that the shapes will lie smoothly when turned right side out.

STEP 4: Turn right side out and press well to make the edge knife sharp.

STEP 5: Mark a square in the center *very lightly* with pencil or chalk for the pillow form.

STEP 6: Topstitch over this line, leaving part of one side open for stuffing.

STEP 7: Stuff in the pillow form.

STEP 8: Finish the final line of topstitching, pushing the form as far away from the stitching as is possible.

STEP 9: Press in the seams at the final edge to be finished as cleanly as possible, and ladder-stitch the final opening at the side together invisibly.

If you wish to put a piping between the pillow and the flange, the flange has to be cut separately from the body of the pillow. This is more complicated both to cut and to sew because you have to make a border similar to a picture frame, allowing exact turnings on pillow and frame, and you must stitch accurately. The flanged border can be of the same

fabric as the center or of a contrasting fabric. The pillow form can be rectangular or even circular and set in an appropriately shaped frame. In the photograph on page 47, the center of the pillow was made of fabric different from the Greek key border which was mitered at the corners. A print on the fabric itself—such as a wavy curve or a geometric zigzag—will often suggest the shape of the flange.

A flanged pillow can be cut in 2 pieces, front and back. Seam around the edge, leaving a space to turn. Turn right side out, and topstitch a centered shape the size of the pillow form through and through. Leave one side of the square unstitched to insert the form.

FLANGED-EDGE PILLOW

The inspiration for this pillow (shown on page 47) with a wide, separate flanged edge was some red and gold, neoclassic fabric that my husband, Keith, found in an antiques shop. This English Regency fabric, which had been cut into strips, dates from the early part of the nineteenth century. I already had a small square of heavy gold satin, but the color was a little too bright to blend with the Regency ribbon. I also found a rather chic trimming of red dots on gold that had the right Regency look as a decoration to go between the ribbon and the body of the pillow, but again, the gold of the braid needed to be murkier. To produce the right effect I dipped both satin and trim in a strong brew of black tea for about five minutes. Beige dye can also do the trick.

Because the Regency ribbon was so wide, I felt the pillow itself should not be too big. There was just enough ribbon to complete the border, allowing for matching and mitering at the corners—which can be tricky with a Greek key pattern. Because there was so little of the gold satin, the ribbon and pillow had to be backed with another gold fabric that did not have to match quite so crucially.

METHOD

STEP 1: To make this pillow, I first cleaned the Regency border of threads, dabbed it very gently with distilled water to remove surface dirt, and pressed it. There were some blemishes and repairs, but that is hardly surprising as the fabric was almost two hundred years old!

STEP 2: I placed the border on the square body of the pillow, centering the pattern and matching as well as possible the mitering of the corners.

STEP 3: I sewed the strips in place with a topstitch.

STEP 4: I topstitched the narrow dotted trimming over the join by machine. This completed the front of the pillow.

STEP 5: Using the front of the pillow as a pattern, complete with the flange of Regency fabric, I cut the back from a gold-colored furnishing cotton.

STEP 6: Then I seamed around the edge of the back and front, taking a tiny seam so as to have as much of the Regency border showing, and leaving a 12-inch (30-cm) opening.

STEP 7: I topstitched through and through at the side of the dotted trimming, leaving a space open almost the whole of one side.

STEP 8: Through the open space I inserted a down-filled pillow form—made exactly the right size.

STEP 9: I pinned the fourth side by the dotted trim, then topstitched through and through, trapping the pillow interior in place.

STEP 10: I hand-sewed the final outside edge using a ladder stitch.

BOUDOIR PILLOWS

Small white or cream-colored pillows are a traditional way to dress a bed. Boudoir pillows should be ultrafeminine and lacy, filled with the best down—unless you have the misfortune to be allergic to down. Tiny ruffled or embroidered pillows can be stuffed with lavender to make a sachet.

Collect antique vintage household linens, hand-embroidered doilies, tray cloths, and napkins to transform into these delicate pillows. If an heirloom embroidered pillow slip wears out, save the lace edging to use on a boudoir pillow. Hang on to scraps of lace and pieces of eyelet embroidery; you don't need a great deal of yardage for these small, frothy confections. Guipure, Venise, Nottingham, and many other varieties of lace, white braids, white fringes, and pearls are all useful for pillow making. (See Lace on page 19 and in the glossary.)

It is helpful to keep a library of white and off-white goods such as sateen, satin, linens of various weights, velveteen, and ottoman. Save pure cotton white sheets once the centers get worn out. They can serve as backing or cover the interiors of pillows.

Buy interesting white and cream ribbons when you see them. Narrow white or pastel-colored satin ribbon looks romantic threaded through crisp white eyelet edging. White grosgrain ribbon is useful to gather or fold into unpressed pleats to make a ruffle for a boudoir pillow. Picot-edged white or pastel ribbons made of taffeta or satin, wide or narrow, have a charming, old-fashioned look. Accent boudoir pillows with mother-of-pearl buttons to give them a sheen.

If you want the pillows to be washable, make sure all the trimmings can be laundered. Make boudoir pillows with sham backs so they can be removed easily. Fasten the shams with unusual white buttons, such as fancy mother-of pearl buttons in offbeat shapes, old-fashioned white cotton cloth-covered buttons, or thread-covered buttons that were used on household linens in the past.

Vintage linens often have stains but they can be treated with suitable stain-removing products or dabbed gently with distilled water (a trick used by museum conservationists), then patted dry with a clean cotton rag. Inevitably some stains are unremovable. These can often be disguised with a ribbon bow, a rosette, or a border of ribbon. Use your imagination to disguise any blemishes and make the pil-

low more interesting in the process. As a last resort, some of the fabric can be cut away and the raw edge covered with lace, leaving any fancy edging in tact.

All the boudoir pillows in the photograph below were made from vintage household linens, attic scraps, or fabric left over from previous sewing projects. The instructions for making the pillows that follow here and in the following chapter therefore do not include specific materials, but are suggestions to spark your own ideas. Instructions for the round ruched pillow (at the top right in the photograph below) begin on page 80, and for the angel pillow (in the center of the photograph), on page 85.

A selection of boudoir pillows clustered on a nineteenth-century four-poster bed shows, clockwise from bottom left, a pillow made from a square linen embroidered dressing table mat surrounded with beige guipure lace; a red-piped circular pillow made from a remnant of white-on-white quilting; a circular lace-edged pillow with a hand-worked doily that combines crochet, ribbon embroidery, and drawn-thread work on handkerchief linen; an "angel" pillow (see pages 82–83); an oblong eyelet piped and ruffled pillow (opposite, top); a circular glazed chintz ruched pillow with glossy white moss fringe around a crocheted doily center (see page 83); a beige linen oblong pillow made from a crochet-edged mat for a vanity table (opposite, bottom); a square oyster heavy silk satin pillow embellished with a delicate hand-embroidered doily and edged with a tiny ruffle (see page 59); a lawn lavender sachet made from the valence of a frayed embroidered undercurtain (flat, center); an oval pillow designed around a doily with tatted lace (see page 83).

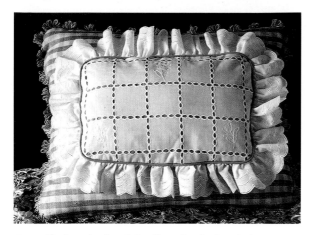

An ruffled eyelet boudoir pillow, backed and piped with blue cotton.

EYELET PILLOW

The boudoir pillow shown above has an eyelet ruffle set on a body made of embroidered eyelet and is backed with plain blue cotton. The piping between the ruffle and the body of the pillow is of the same fabric.

MATERIALS

Pillow fabric: The amount will vary according to the size pillow you want to make. For a small eyelet pillow such as the one pictured, you need only ½ yard (46 cm) of fabric.

For this pillow you will also need ½ yard (46 cm) of solid fabric for backing the eyelet and for making piping.

If the ruffle is to be of the same fabric as the front of the pillow you will need ¾ yard (69 cm) of fabric instead of ½ yard. However, at fabric and craft stores you can buy many pretty ready-made eyelet ruffles already gathered onto a heading. Measure around the edge of the pillow and buy to the nearest ½ yard (46 cm). You can also make your own ruffled eyelet if you buy ungathered eyelet edging, in which case buy three times the length of the edge of your pillow. Unruffled eyelet edging often has an uneven raw edge. Make sure that yours will be wide enough when you have taken off a complete ½-inch (13-mm) seam.

You will need narrow piping filler.

Pillow interior: As the pillow shown is small, you may find it easier to make your own interior from ticking filled with down or fiberfill.

For this pillow (which was made from a scrap I had kept in the attic for so many years I've forgotten where it came from), parts of the eyelet had been machine embroidered using a chain stitch. Fabric that you select can be plain, embroidered by hand, or embroidered by machine. One way to do machine embroidery with a loose, flowing line effect follows.

MACHINE EMBROIDERY

METHOD

STEP 1: Place the part to be embroidered in an embroidery hoop.

STEP 2: With light pencil strokes, sketch the design. Do not aim for a tight, exact design using this method.

Among my hoard of vintage linens was this embroidered linen place mat, which inspired a small pillow trimmed with lace that was dipped in tea to make the right beige color.

STEP 3: Thread the machine in whatever color you wish to use. Take the foot off the machine.

STEP 4: Set the hoop under the needle, then move the hoop so that the stitches form a design. You will be using the straight stitches (rather than chain stitches) like a pencil, in free form. You may have to experiment to get the tension correct.

PILLOW ASSEMBLY

METHOD

STEP 1: Once you have your embroidery, cut the front and the back (which need not be embroidered). Cut the solid fabric to go underneath and show through the eyelet (if you are using eyelet).

STEP 2: Machine-stitch the front to the solid fabric all around the perimeter.

STEP 3: Cut bias strips for the piping from the solid fabric. Join the bias seams and press them open. Using a zipper foot, make the piping (see Step 4 on page 43).

STEP 4: Sew the piping to the front of pillow and finish the seam of the piping on the bias as for the basic pillow (see Diagrams 12 through 17 on page 35).

STEP 5: For the ruffle, cut the exact amount you will need of ready-made eyelet. If you are using unruffled eyelet edging, cut three times the length of the outside of the pillow.

STEP 6: Make a French seam in the eyelet ruffling to have the ruffle clean-finished on both sides. Do this by making a 1/8-inch (3-mm) seam on the right side, then turning it to the wrong side and taking a 1/4-inch (7-mm) seam, trapping the raw edges of the first seam inside.

STEP 7: If you are going to gather the ruffle, fold the ruffle into quarters and mark it with notches and pins as pictured in Diagram 2 on page 45.

Gather the ruffle. Pin it to the front of the pillow and arrange the gathers evenly.

STEP 8: To sew the ruffle onto the front of pillow, use the zipper foot so that you can get right up close to the piping. Sew with the wrong side of the front pillow uppermost, with the piping underneath and the ruffles below the piping. This way you can use the stitch holding the piping as a guide, and go a hairbreadth beyond it.

STEP 9: Join the front to the back, still using the zipper foot and tucking the ruffle inside carefully as you stitch (see Diagram 3, page 45).

STEP 10: Turn the pillow right side out, stuff in the pillow interior, and stitch up the opening by hand (see Diagrams 18 through 20, page 36).

LACE DOILY AND SATIN PILLOW

See the square pillow at the bottom right of the photograph on page 50 and the photo on page 59. The lace doily that inspired the construction of this pillow was so cobweb-fine and perfect that it looked as if it had been made by fairy hands—though it was, in fact, part of the cache of household linens made by one of my maiden great-aunts. It had probably never been used. I selected the oyster-colored silk-faced heavy satin for this pillow because it enhanced the delicacy of the doily.

Keep in mind that cutting heavy satin is difficult because the cloth curls. To prevent this you can use weights or anchor the fabric to a cutting table with adhesive tape. Make sure that you have smooth fingernails when using satin or any precious silky fabrics because any roughness can snag on silk satin.

As I mentioned in the section Ruffles earlier in this chapter, ruffles can look very elegant and not too frilly if they are tiny. To make tiny ruffled frills, you must cut enough bias satin 2 inches (5 cm) wide to go twice around the outside edge of the pillow. (This frill is so narrow and the fabric is so heavy that the usual 3-to-1 gathering is too tricky to sew.) Then proceed as for regular ruffles.

If there is a center to the doily that needs emphasis, as there was in this one, it is nice to sew on a tiny pearl button as a finishing touch.

EMBROIDERED LINEN AND LACE PILLOW

See the square pillow at bottom far left of the photograph on page 50 and in the photo on page 51. I got the idea for making this pillow by observing the play of cream and natural colors combined together. The small mat on this pillow, 5 inches (13 cm) square, is made of natural linen with a drawn-thread hem and simple embroidery in the corners. I found a scrap of beige guipure lace that had been stored in my attic for years. I believe the lace had at one point been dipped in tea and used on a fancy dress costume. There was—to the millimeter—exactly enough lace to go around the edge of the little mat. I made simple inverted pleats at each corner rather than mitering the lace and running into the problem of mismatching the design of the lace. The seam in the lace is well hidden under one of the pleats.

The body of the pillow is modern ecru-colored linen, not so fine, but near enough to match that of the embroidered mat. The piping is made from heavy cream-colored ottoman.

On a pillow as small as this, planning and accuracy of the details are enormously important. It is vital to place the design of the lace so that there are exactly the same number of scallops on each side of the pillow because the slightest asymmetry will be very obvious. It is worthwhile spending time placing and pinning the various elements until they are as perfect as you can make them.

USING RIBBON FOR PILLOWS

Ribbons come in hundreds of varieties (see Ribbon, page 24). If you have access to a store that specializes in ribbon, such as those in New York's garment district, the merchandise can be truly inspiring.

However, most craft and fabric stores stock a variety of plain or striped grosgrain ribbons, which are the most versatile of all to use. There are many beautiful and original ways to use ribbons.

Ribbon can be gathered or pleated and used as ruffles. Remember to buy ribbon ½ inch (13 mm) wider than you want the ruffle, for seam allowance. If you want to introduce two colors into your color scheme, gather two ribbons as ruffles. Or you can sew a narrow ribbon on top of another wider ribbon to produce a striped effect and introduce a second color. Test with a small piece to see how the ribbon gathers. You may find that 2-to-1 gathering is plenty.

Ribbon is wonderful to use as a braid, topstitched onto a pillow front as a decoration. It's best to miter the ribbon at the corners if the pillow is a square or rectangular shape. You can also use ribbon as a border for needlepoint. Make a habit of saving ribbon scraps. They will come in handy when you want to thread ribbon through eyelet, or to make bows, fancy rosettes, or for instance, a Maltese cross motif to be sewn into the center of a pillow and held in place by a large domed pearl button. Make rosettes by stitching along one edge of the ribbon and pulling the gathering tight. Rosettes can be single-, double-, or even triple-layered, and can also be held in place with a ribbon-covered or jeweled button. White, pale pink, and pale blue satin ribbon can be made into tiny roses to embellish boudoir pillows.

WEAVING RIBBONS

You can also use ribbons as a fabric by weaving them into a pillow. I first saw this done when a friend of mine, designer Sheila Kotur, gave my two girls dainy heart-shaped "tooth fairy" pillows of pastel-colored, picot-edged taffeta and flower-figured ribbons. These lovely pillows decorated my daughters' beds for years. We still have one tucked away, two decades later.

Recently I made a more masculine-looking checkerboard pillow using the same principle. I used black and white grosgrain ribbon for the board, and a dark green moiré ribbon as the framing in a sort of imitation of wood graining. I had a scrap of green felt which I used on the back.

CHECKERBOARD PILLOW

MATERIALS

4 yards (3.7 m) of black 1½-inch-wide (4-cm) grosgrain ribbon

4 yards (3.7 m) of white 1½-inch (4-cm) grosgrain ribbon

4 yards (3.7 m) of 2-inch-wide (5-cm) moiré ribbon in your choice of color, for framing and side gusset

½ yard (46 cm) of fabric for pillow back. This should match as closely as possible the color of the 2-inch (5-cm) framing ribbon. It could be felt, which comes in many colors (real checkerboards are often backed with felt), or baize, or ottoman, which echoes the ribbed effect of the grosgrain. The advantage of using felt is that it can be topstitched without turning in a seam.

½ yard (46 cm) of muslin, ticking, or sheeting to make the pillow stuffing case

Stuffing for pillow: For a flat shape like this, fiberfill in the form of yard goods—such as that used for quilting—is best, and it can be topped up with feather down

Thread to match the framing ribbon

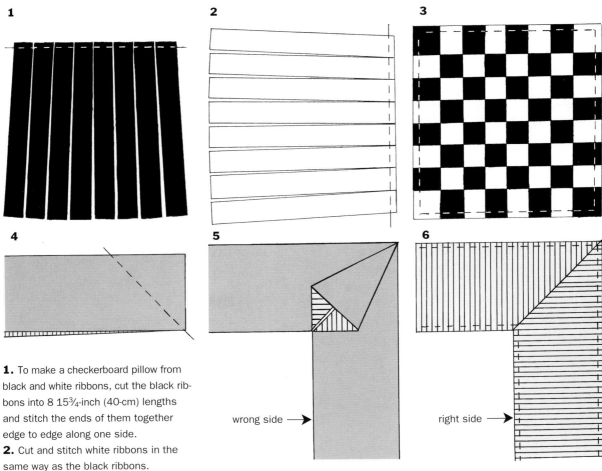

1. To make a checkerboard pillow from black and white ribbons, cut the black ribbons into 8 15¾-inch (40-cm) lengths and stitch the ends of them together edge to edge along one side.

2. Cut and stitch white ribbons in the same way as the black ribbons.

3. Interweave both sets of ribbons to form a checkerboard design, then secure the oppposite ends of the ribbons with a row of stitching.

4. To make a mitered corner when using wide ribbon, fold the ribbon back on itself when you come to the outside corner. Stitch from this corner at a 45-degree angle on the wrong side of the ribbon as shown.

5. Press the seam open on the wrong side. Make sure the folds are equally distributed on the slanting seam.

6. Topstitch the ribbon in place.

METHOD

STEP 1: Cut the black and white ribbons into eight 15¾-inch (40-cm) lengths.

STEP 2: Line up all the black ribbon strips side by side and machine-stitch them along the ends. Similarly, line up the white ribbons and stitch.

STEP 3: Interweave the ribbons to form a checkerboard. When woven, topstitch at opposite sides to hold the ribbons in place.

STEP 4: With exactly matching thread, top stitch at the edge of the 2-inch (5-cm) framing ribbon sewing it right onto the checkered ribbons, and mitering the corners. As the grosgrain ribbon tends to slip about, you may have to pin the corners first, stitching the miters on the wrong side (pressing them open as in Diagram 4), then topstitching.

STEP 5: Edge-stitch on the right-side 2-inch (5-cm) ribbon onto the framing ribbon to make the side gusset (the insert or side piece) of the pillow.

STEP 6: Cut a 16¼-inch (41-cm) square from felt for the back of the pillow. As it is felt, only ⅛-inch seam allowance is needed for topstitching.

STEP 7: Topstitch the gusset ribbon onto the felt back of the pillow, leaving one side open for turning and stuffing.

STEP 8: To make the stuffing form, cut 2 pieces of muslin or ticking 17 inches (43 cm) square. Cut a gusset strip 3 inches (8 cm) wide by 1-yard 5-inches (165 cm), which is 16 by 4 inches plus ½-inch seam allowance. The gusset strip can be pieced because it will not show. Seam the pieces to make the pillow form leaving an opening for the stuffing. Cut fiberfill into 16-inch (41-cm) squares and stuff it into the pillow form. Top off with feathers or wadding as needed to fill out the form and make it firm. Sew up the opening.

STEP 9: Stuff the pillow form into your checkerboard pillow exterior and make sure it fits neatly into the corners. Topstitch the opening by machine, pinning it first.

STRIPES

Stripes are fun to play around with on pillows. Within a simple square there are many ways to cut the stripes so that they form unexpected and unique designs. The diagrams on page 56 show ten different stripe ideas. You can invent many others depending on the size and design of the stripe.

Allow extra fabric when making striped pillows if there is a lot of matching and mitering involved. If the stripes are one-sided in design, and have a right and a wrong side, allow extra fabric because you will need more goods to match the stripes. If the fabric is exactly the same on the front as on the back, as in certain woven stripes, cutting is easier and takes less yardage than with printed stripes.

Piping, if part of your design, can be solid fabric, cord on a tape, or the striped fabric used on the bias.

SQUARE STRIPED PILLOW

METHOD

STEP 1: First determine the size of your pillow. Then cut this shape in paper—brown wrapping paper is fine for this purpose. Mark the design you want to use on the paper so that you can adjust the proportions to your satisfaction. For designs such as those illustrated in the series of diagrams, make every angle exactly either 90 or 45 degrees in order to match the stripes correctly. The pillow corners can be slivered off once the mitered stripes have been stitched as long as this does not distort the design.

STEP 2: On the pillow pattern, indicate the direction of the stripes. If the stripe is large, mark the actual stripe onto your pattern pieces. As you get more experienced, you will be able to eliminate some of these stages.

The diagrams on this page show ten different ways to place stripes on a pillow.

STEP 3: Cut the paper pattern along the actual lines of the seams, minus seam allowance, separating the parts.

STEP 4: Cut new patterns using the first pattern pieces as templates, adding ½-inch (13-mm) seam allowances on all sides and marking the direction and position of the stripes.

STEP 5: Lay the patterns on the fabrics, draw around them, and cut the pieces in cloth. Take plenty of time to cut the shapes accurately, making sure the stripes will match. That way the stitching will be easier.

STEP 6: Cut, make, and attach any piping you may need. If you have designed a pillow with a small central square on top of a larger square (such as shown in Diagrams 47, 51 and 52), make a pattern for the large square and for the small square. You will find it easier to put a piping around the edge of the small square, then to topstitch the small square on top of the large square, stitching in the groove between the pillow and the piping. Once the topstitching is done, the fabric underneath the small square can be cut away if necessary.

STEP 7: Pin the pieces together before stitching to make sure that all the stripes match. There is a logical way to seam the stripes: Join the quarter shapes first, then join the halves together in one seam. Check each seam as you go, and correct any that have slipped out of match. You will be working on the true bias most of the time, and bias fabric tends to slip and slide. If you do not trust your machine stitching using pins, baste the seams.

STEP 8: The same piping used on a small applied square can be used around the edge of the pillow. Before adding the outside piping, sliver off the corners as for a regular knife-edged pillow (see Diagram 6 on page 33), unless this interferes noticeably with the stripe design. As a general rule, slivering off the corners is a more desirable option than having the corners stick out.

STEP 9: Cut the back of the pillow. The back can be made exactly like the front, making the pillow usable on either side, or you can simply have stripes running vertically on the back. An alternative is to use the fabric used for piping for the back.

STEP 10: Sew the back to the front, leaving a space to turn. Turn, stuff in pillow form, and ladder-stitch up the opening.

TRIMMING

Pillows can be given the ultimate finishing touch by the judicious use of passementerie. Here are some ideas:

BRAID

Flat braids, sometimes called tapes, can usually be sewn on by machine. There is also a large category of braids and gimps that are more three-dimensional, being plaited or constructed in such a way that a machine stitch would mar their effect, so this type of braid is best sewn on by hand. Many of them are flexible—like a plait—and can be used in circles and ovals, unlike the flat tape braids. The best technique is to lay the braid onto the fabric, pin it in place, and take tiny invisible stitches underneath to hold the braid firmly onto the pillow.

Braids and fancy ribbons are sometimes hand-stitched over the perimeter of a knife-edged pillow. I have seen this on an old French wine-colored silk velvet pillow with an applied 1½-inch (4-cm) antique gold braid. This technique gives a three-dimensional effect similar to a gusset. The pillow was made before sewing machines were invented. If the squared-off look of a gusset is needed, it is easier to insert a gusset to which you have already applied the braid by machine. But keep in mind this caution: Seam allowances must be accurate or you will catch the braid by mistake in the seams.

Left: This heart-shaped woven-ribbon "tooth fairy" pillow was given to my daughter Jassy by designer Sheila Kotur.

Right: This small oyster satin boudoir pillow applied with a doily of delicate vintage lace made by my great-aunt has a diminutive self-ruffle.

Below: A simple stripe in black and red on white canvas, mitered to form a design and piped at the edge in plain red.

Right: A pillow made of terry toweling gives a feeling of comfort to a bathroom. This one is trimmed with washable lace and ribbon.

Left: This checkerboard pillow was inspired by woven pillows given by a friend to my children. The black and white grosgrain ribbons are readily available in craft and fabric stores.

CORD AND ROPE

Silky corded trimmings give a rich and sumptuous finish to the edges of pillows. Cords and ropes are similar in construction, though a cord is a thinner form of rope. Both can be used in pillow making, depending on the scale of the pillow. Some cords and ropes come attached to a tape for insertion. Rope or cord that is not attached to a tape has to be sewn on by hand, which takes more time than trapping a cord in the seam.

The one problem with cord and rope, whether on a tape or not, is finishing where the end meets the beginning. Much depends on the way the rope is made. I usually put the join in the center of the bottom of the pillow where it will be the least obvious, unless the cords are to be trapped into each of the corners. The best way to finish the ends invisibly is to interweave the ends of one cord with the beginnings of the other and trap the unraveled ends of both in the seam. The interweaving has to be done by hand.

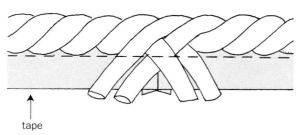

tape

To join the ends of a cord on tape invisibly, allow an inch of cord beyond the notch at the center bottom of the pillow. Separate the cord from the tape with small scissors. Allow ¼ inch (6 cm) beyond the notch on the tape and seam the ends together. Untwist the strands of cord, interweaving them as shown, then catch the cord ends with a row of stitching.

Another way of finishing is simply to overlap the cords. However, if they are thick, this can end up being bulky where they overlap. Some cords have a central cotton core, which can be cut away to make overlapping the cords less cumbersome to stitch.

Cord or rope can be hand-sewn onto the front of a pillow to add a decorative touch, to cover the seam between a piece of needlepoint and the fram-

ing fabric, or to form curls at the corners of pillows to add passementerie embellishment, as shown in the diagram on page 70. Or cords can be looped at corners, and the ends disguised by being trapped into the corners. (See the small double loops at the corners of the beaded red needlepoint pillow in the photograph on page 30.)

There are many varieties of cords and ropes available at the decorative fabric houses. They are made of silk, cotton, and other blends of fibers. Some are all one color, others are multicolored. You may find a cording in just the right combination of colors for you, and when you do, let your imagination tell you how best to apply it. (See Cord, page 24, and Rope, page 25.)

FRINGES

I have seen almost every kind of fringe there is used on pillows, from long leather fringes on a rugged leather pillow to knotted crystal bead fringe on an antique beaded needlepoint pillow.

Of all the fringes I've worked with, I've found that moss (or brush) fringe is one of the most useful. It is most effective to double it up to give it extra fullness.

Overall, most fringes are constructed on a heading that can be trapped in the seam at the edge of the pillow. If a design calls for the fringe to be attached on the outside, right near the edge of the pillow, it is best sewn on by hand after the rest of the pillow is completed. (See Fringe, page 24.)

TASSELS

There are a number of common uses for tassels. On square or rectangular pillows, tassels usually emerge from the folds of a French corner where the loop at the top of the tassel is trapped. (See Tassels, page 25.)

Or sometimes a tassel can be placed in the center of a large floor cushion. To make the tassel look functional, it should appear to be pulling the center toward the back, like tufting in upholstery. For a nice finish, surround the ends of the tassel's loop with a rosette. Tassels are usually set into the center of the round ends of cylindrical pillows that are placed at the ends of sofas. (See Cylindrical Pillows, page 82, and the photographs on pages 20 and 47.)

PILLOWS OF TOWELING

For a bathroom, a pillow made of any kind of toweling gives a comfortable, warm touch. I like to recycle old terry towels, using the unworn parts to make a pillow. As a present for my eldest daughter, a friend sent a tiny pillow made of soft, cotton diaper cloth, edged with a ruffle of checked cotton. To create a personal touch, she embroidered a message on it. The pillow looked very much at home sitting on a terry-covered slipper chair in the bathroom.

MATERIAL

Pillow Fabric: For the pillow photographed in a bathroom, I used exactly what I had in my house—an old white towel that had been stained in one place with paint.
1 yard (1 m) of flat lace edging
A short piece—1 yard (1 m) would suffice—of washable satin ribbon, which I laid on top of the lace
2 yards (1.8 m) of highly washable narrow polyester swag trimming
Washable polyester fiberfill

METHOD

STEP 1: Cut the pillow shape, square or oblong, according to the size and shape of your towel.

STEP 2: Make an interior casing from washable sheeting the same size as the pillow. Fill it with washable polyester fiberfill. Feathers and down smell when wet and are not as easily washed. Terry is a difficult cloth to put a zipper into, and is too thick to make a satisfactory sham, so it is best to make the whole pillow washable.

STEP 3: Pin the lace trimming onto the front of the terry pillow front diagonally from corner to corner. Make sure you place the best side up. (Always establish the right and wrong side of lace before you stitch. One side always looks better than the other and is finished more smoothly.) If there is a strong motif in the trimming, pin from the middle to the outside. Do not stretch the trimming or the pillow will buckle.

STEP 4: Topstitch the lace trimming onto the pillow front. You may need to stitch on both sides or to stitch through the center, which will be covered by the ribbon.

STEP 5: Pin on the ribbon and topstitch it along both sides.

STEP 6: Pin on the polyester swag trimming. As you did with the lace, establish a motif in the center first and pin out from there. Topstitch the trimming so the stitch shows as little as possible.

STEP 7: Stitch the trimming to the edge of the pillow. I used the same swag fringe on the edge as for the diagonal, trapping part of it in the seam and letting just one side of scallops show. With any trimming that has an obvious shape, pin it first to make sure the motifs are centered in the center of each side.

STEP 8: Join the front of the pillow to the back, going a shade further than the stitch used to apply the trimming and leaving an opening for turning.

STEP 9: Turn right side out, and stuff in the filler pillow, and ladder-stitch the opening.

CHAPTER 5

FRAMED AND PAINTED PILLOWS

There are a number of ways to enhance a unique piece of fabric or embroidery to emphasize its quality and design. One of my favorite techniques is what I call framing. This is particularly appropriate for use on antique needlepoint and painted pillows. Framing is also appropriate to surround scraps of fur, precious pieces of brocade, antique chintz, and handmade needlework, and as a setting for embroidered emblems, such as those found on blazers.

Needlepoint is very much with us as a craft today. Modern needlepoint has a special look and place in our lives, and is used on belts, bags, luggage tags—everything from Christmas tree ornaments to ecclesiastical hassocks. And much of our modern needlepoint ends up on pillows—sometimes pre-designed from a kit, sometimes, more interestingly, created for a special friend with a personal message.

Though needlepoint has been with us since Jacobean days, it developed in the last two hundred years because of the burgeoning economy brought on by the industrial revolution. Many European and American ladies no longer had to be part of the work force and so had time on their hands to devote to any number of intricate crafts, of which needlepoint was but one. Quilting, patchwork, and painting theorem pictures on velvet

were others. During the nineteenth century a tremendous amount of needlepoint was created for pictures as well as for useful objects, from tea cozies to carpets. Many pieces of needlepoint have survived from the nineteenth century and can be made up into wonderful pillows, though good antique needlepoint nowadays tends to be costly, needs repairing, and is becoming less easy to find. I have a large needlepoint picture embroidered by my great-grandmother in 1850 from her own design, in a frame carved by my great-grandfather.

Overall, there is something particularly appealing about old needlepoint. The colors of the wool yarns are pleasantly faded and can tone in well with almost any but the most starkly modern room. If, however, you look on the reverse side of antique needlepoint, the original, often garish colors—especially the later Victorian pieces when the use of chemical dyes produced vivid colors—can be quite startling.

Some antique needlepoint pieces are complete squares, requiring nothing more than a handsome cord edge, a back, and stuffing to make a wonderful pillow. There is more of a challenge in using the types of remnants that may look a little forlorn to begin with but can be framed to become little works of art. Because of the subdued coloring, caused by use and fading, antique needlepoint

Shown in an upholstered child's chair are four tiny pillows made from scraps of antique needlepoint. The smallest piece is 3½ inches by 5 inches (9 cm by 13 cm) but the velvet framing allows the final pillow to be 7½ inches by 9 inches (19 cm by 23 cm) in size.

often needs livening up a bit, rather in the way a subtle watercolor needs elegant French matting to enhance its impact. In both cases it is the framing that helps to bring out the best in the work.

Most pieces of needlepoint are made up into square or oblong pillows. Occasionally you will find round, oval, or shield-shaped needlepoint. The needlepoint piece itself dictates the final size of the pillow. As a general rule, for a piece of needlepoint that is, say, 8 inches by 10 inches (20 cm by 25 cm), the pillow itself and its interior should be 13 inches by 15 inches (33 cm by 38 cm).

Because there are often as many as six different elements involved in making up each framed needlepoint pillow, keep as many scraps of fabric as you can, and also keep trimming scraps. As I advised earlier, this way you can build of a library of materials from which to choose. Keep the scraps together according to their color. A cupboard where you can see the colors at a glance is useful. Otherwise, use cardboard boxes of the sort that moving companies use for books. They can be clearly labeled on the sides and the top and can be stacked.

For many years I have observed the way Keith creates a frame of fabric around old pieces of needlepoint to make a pillow. Here are a few hints.

ELEMENTS NEEDED TO MAKE A PILLOW FROM A PIECE OF NEEDLEPOINT

• A *needlepoint* piece.
• A *pillow interior* chosen with the size and shape of the needlepoint in mind plus the amount of its framing border.
• *Cording, piping, or braid* to sew around the edge of the needlepoint, to form a logical fence between the embroidery and its framing fabric. If the needlepoint is a little drab, choose the color of the edging from one of the colors in the needlepoint but slightly more vivid in color. If you select cord, make sure it is a narrow one so it doesn't overpower the needlepoint. If you are going to make your own piping, ottoman is the ideal fabric because its ribs on the bias resemble cording. Use a

narrow filler cord. The same ottoman fabric can be used to back the pillow.
• *Fabric to frame the needlepoint.* This fabric covers the front of the pillow, but only a border of it will actually show framing the needlepoint. Choose a fabric that is different in color or texture from the trimming you put around the edge of the needlepoint. Because old needlepoint is normally made of all-natural fiber such as wool, though it might include silk, metallic thread, or beading, it is a good idea to choose a natural-fiber framing. Silk or cotton taffeta, velveteen, and ottoman are all good choices. You will need enough for the size of the needlepoint plus 3 inches to 5 inches (8 cm to 13 cm) more on all four sides.
• *Cord, fringe, or piping to go around the outside edge of the pillow.* Choose a third color from within the needlepoint design. For this outside edge use a fatter cord or piping, or a fringe with some body. To determine the amount needed, measure around the pillow interior and add at least 2 inches (5 cm) for overlapping the ends. This should be sewn onto the pillow front.
• *The pillow back.* This may be the same fabric as the front of the pillow or the same as one of the piping fabrics, but it is often more interesting to use a different but blending-colored cloth with some body to it. Ottoman and velvet are ideal, as is a heavy furnishing fabric in imitation of solid-colored needlepoint called gros point. But there are many other fabric possibilities, depending on what you have among your scraps. You will need the same amount of fabric as for the front framing.

In order to make your choices, lay out the fabric options from your library together with the needlepoint. Play with them, placing them in proportion to the pillow. Do this in daylight since colors change considerably in artificial light. Consider all the possibilities and then make your final selection—basing your decisions on the colors in the needlepoint and the room for which the pillow is intended. Make sure you have enough of each fabric for its purpose.

If you cannot find the right colors, remember

that both fabric and trimming can be hand-dyed at home. To turn white into beige, materials can be dipped in coffee or tea.

If you cannot find a two-tone corded trimming in the right colors ready made, make a double piping (see Double Piping, page 37). Since the needlepoint pillow can be used only on the right side, the problem of the somewhat unsatisfactory look of the back of double piping will not matter.

If, for the sake of the color of the framing, you have to use a thin fabric, back it with muslin or sheeting. If the needlepoint is badly worn, it should also be backed.

Tiny pillows that need very little fabric and trimming are as appealing as large pillows. I was fascinated to learn that Doctor Johnson's famous 1755 *Dictionary of the English Language* mentions "cushionets" as small cushions. Save every scrap of old needlepoint. Small pieces of needlepoint can always be framed to make them look important. (See the photograph on page 62.) Wood shavings make ideal stuffing for tiny needlepoint pillows, turning them into pincushions.

Save any scraps of blank canvas too, and keep a supply of different colored wool yarns in case you have to make repairs. Often even the black parts of needlepoint fade to a dark brown, so keep several shades of black, charcoal, and brown yarn on hand. Repair needlepoint before making it into a pillow, but don't overrepair it. As is the case with overrestored furniture, overrestored needlepoint can lose its charm. Try to keep the patina of age, and leave those little signs of use that reveal the fabric's history.

The success in framing a piece of needlepoint lies in the selection of the details and the perfection of assembling them. Do not overdo the use of passementerie trimmings. A caution: The temptation, in decorating as in fashion, is to be finicky about matching colors exactly. However—and this is a subtle point—a pillow may be more pleasing if colors are insinuated rather than exactly matched. You don't want a pillow to look like a mass-produced item bought from a catalogue or at the local mall. A pillow is more satisfying if it gives the effect of having developed, imperfections and all, over the years. Discriminating color and unlikely fabric variations require sophistication, but the result is far more fascinating than the all-too-obvious choices. And remember, with experience and taste, all rules can be broken.

FRAMED PILLOW

METHOD

STEP 1: Once you have assembled the various ingredients to make your framed pillow, cut the complete front piece, which will frame the needlepoint or painted pillow.

STEP 2: Cut the back.

STEP 3: Cut the piping for edging the needlepoint.

STEP 4: Cut the piping for the edge of the pillow.

STEP 5: Sew the trimming around the edge of the needlepoint.

STEP 6: Pin the edged needlepoint onto the pillow front, tucking the raw seams underneath. Cut away excess seams, and stagger them if they are very thick. The object is to avoid having the impression of a seam show through on the finished pillow. If the needlepoint has a one-way design, lift the center of the design 1 inch (3 cm) higher than the center of the pillow front, to take care of "pillow slouch." As is standard when framing a picture, keep the margin at the bottom wider than the margins at the sides and top.

STEP 7: Using a zipper foot, machine-stitch slowly and carefully in the groove between the piping and the needlepoint, making sure all the seams are well tucked underneath. If you are using a flat braid instead of piping, topstitch the needlepoint onto the pillow front, then apply the braid by hand or by machine. If necessary, the fabric beneath the needlepoint can be cut away to make the pillow front lie more smoothly once the stitching is done.

Above: In an English hall porter's chair sits the first painted pillow I had ever seen. This pillow made from a nineteenth-century stenciled painting on velveteen inspired me to try my hand at painting pillows.

Above: These painted pillows were inspired by *Les Fleurs Animées* by Jean-Ignace Grandville, originally published in 1847. The tiny circular pillow was a valentine to Keith from Emma, our eldest daughter.

Top right: This pillow showing two Scotsmen in kilts was a present for Keith. I found the design in a book on Chinese Export porcelain and chose it because Keith is Scottish. I was amused to see that because the plate was painted by a Chinese artist, the Scotsmen have Chinese faces.

Left: Because my husband is from Scotland, he is always on the lookout for Scottish motifs, such as this large piece of needlepoint, which was probably intended as a picture for the wall. The unorthodox choice of a wide plaited braid border, red and pink and green checked surround, and a fine silk taffeta piping and back show that there are many effective framing possibilities.

Above: This faded and worn piece of Victorian needlepoint was given a new appearance with the turquoise ottoman piping border, framed in a red oblong and edged with black moss fringe. The unseen back is of heavy green strié satin.

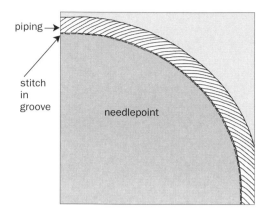

To stitch in the groove when framing a piece of needlepoint, turn all inside seams toward the center. Use a zipper foot and direct the needle into the seam between the piping and the needlepoint.

STEP 8: Sew the trimming to the edge of the front of the pillow.

STEP 9: Sew the completed front of the pillow to the back, leaving an opening for turning.

STEP 10: Turn the pillow, stuff it, and ladder-stitch up the edge.

MODERN NEEDLEPOINT

Most modern needlepoint pieces do not require as elaborate framing as old pieces do, especially incomplete or damaged old needlepoint. Modern colors are less faded, and therefore do not need to be enhanced by a fabric frame. The design itself often incorporates a border of some kind.

USING CORD IN FRAMING

Sometimes cords are used not only to decorate the edge of a pillow but also to decorate the corners of the frame around a piece of needlepoint used on a pillow. First, trap a piece of rope into each corner. Then, as invisibly as possible, sew it in a straight line

toward the corner of the needlepoint. Next, curl the rope into a circle and stitch it in place. Finish by winding thread around the end of the rope to prevent it unraveling, and tucking it invisibly under the circle of rope as you sew (see the diagram at left).

ODD-SHAPED PIECES OF NEEDLEPOINT

Sometimes old pieces of needlepoint are not square or oblong in shape and don't easily lend themselves to pillow shapes. I have had pieces stored away in tissue paper for years, never quite knowing what to do with them. With a little thought, they can be recycled into pillows. Most often they can be framed with piping or braid and mounted onto rectangular pillows. Occasionally you come across arched or shield-shaped pieces that were originally designed to be made into fire screens, but have never been mounted. They can make handsome upright pillows with arched tops.

BELLPULL PILLOW

You might come across a long, narrow strip of antique needlepoint and wonder what on earth to do with it. Originally it would have been intended as a bellpull, dating from the days when servants would be summoned from their downstairs hall. Nowadays bellpulls, if in a good state, may be simply hung on the wall as decoration, but they are often more useful made into pillows.

The bellpull pillow in the photograph on page 71 is not strictly speaking a framed pillow; the fringe around the needlepoint gives a framing effect. If a larger pillow is needed, an oblong piece can be given an edge of piping, cording, or braid, then set on a frame of another fabric.

METHOD

STEP 1: The best way to use a needlepoint bellpull as a pillow is to cut the bellpull into pieces to form an oblong. How long and into how many pieces you cut the needlepoint will depend on the repeat of the design. Make sure that the design of the needlepoint relates from each cut piece to the next, so that the overall effect will be logical when they are joined together to form a rectangle.

STEP 2: Select complementary-colored trimming to form a division between each section. This may be cording on a tape or piping.

STEP 3: Stitch the cording or piping between each piece using a zipper foot and a heavyweight needle (size 16). Then join the pieces together to form a rectangle.

STEP 4: If your oblong is not a standard-size pillow, make your own pillow interior from ticking and stuff it with down or fiberfill.

STEP 5: Sew cord, piping, or fringe all around the outside. This can be the same as the piping between the strips or another complementary color. In the top-left photograph on page 71, the black piping is made from ottoman, and the fringe, saved from another project, is antique. You may find it difficult to sew the outside trimming around the perimeter of the pillow because of the thickness of the cord. To make this easier, cut away ½ inch (13 mm) from the inside filler before you add the outside trimming. When stitching the outside trimming on, go slowly, lifting the machine foot if necessary, otherwise you may break the needle. As a last resort, hand-stitch this part of the operation.

STEP 6: Select, cut, and sew on a backing fabric, of a complementary color or the same fabric as the piping. Again, you will have thick layers of fabric and trimming, so go slowly. Remember to leave an opening for turning.

STEP 7: Turn the needlepoint pillow right side out, stuff with the interior form, and hand-sew the opening using an invisible ladder stitch. Remove excess threads and fluff up the pillow.

FRAMED FUR PILLOW

Real fur is increasingly precious. Fur should be appreciated, enhanced, and glamorized—like the embroidered leopard skins used by priests in ancient Egypt. Don't discard fur. Even a small piece can be made into a pillow.

At the risk of sounding politically incorrect, here are instructions for making a fur pillow. I love animals as much—probably more—than the next person, and I am attracted to the beauty of their fur. But fur is fragile, dries out, and disintegrates. There are many people who have fur coats that they will never wear again—because the coats are falling apart, or because the wearers are intimidated by paint throwers. I have never worn a leopard coat such as the one used for this project, but I see no sin in recycling a coat that will never be worn again and making its fur once more into a thing of beauty.

If you are using an old fur coat, examine it carefully. The size of your pillow will depend on the size of your fur and how much surround you wish to add. Many close-fitting fur coats get smaller higher up the body, so you may have to use the part nearest the hem. If you want to make a pair of cushions to go on either side of a sofa, you may have to make each pillow smaller. If the fur is leopard (as pictured on page 75), ocelot, or deerskin, you will see that the markings have a definite centerline, from which the animal's distinctive pattern flows. This will have to be centered on your pillow. Take plenty of time deciding before you cut anything. You can't afford to make any mistakes. If the front of the coat has a wide turnback that has not been cut into for buttonholes, you may have enough to make two pillows using the fronts, one on each side. You may find that you will have more fur to work with using the sleeves than using the body.

Even if you have only a small piece of fur to use, you can make a pillow look bigger if the fur is surrounded by a frame of another fabric. On the leopard pillow shown in the photograph on page 75, the surround is dark brown sueded cowhide that has the effect of suede.

The method given below can also be used to

Cord can be applied to a pillow in a decorative way.

make a pillow from fake fur. There are some beautiful printed and woven flat-fur fabrics to be found. However, high-pile fake furs, though ingeniously made, are nowhere as nice as the real thing.

MATERIALS

A scrap of fur: in this case part of a worn-out coat

Framing fabric: such as dark brown sueded cowhide

Fabric for the back of pillow: heavy antiqued furnishing velvet

Flat braid to cover fur-to-suede seam: I used a black and gold Greek key design.

Piping or cord for the perimeter: here a black/brown/ cream cord on tape

Pillow interior and extra fluff for corners. You may not be able to decide the size until you have examined the fur you have selected carefully.

Machine threads to match braid

Number 18 machine needles, for heavyweight fabric

Zipper foot. If you can find a Teflon-coated foot, which prevents sticking, use that for stitching the fur to the suede.

Heavy buttonhole thread, leather needle, and thimble for hand-stitching the side of pillow

A blade or knife for cutting

Rubber cement or double-sided adhesive tape to hold the fur in place

METHOD

STEP 1: If you are going to use the body of a coat, use small scissors to carefully snip the stitches that hold the lining in place around the neck, down the fronts, and around the hem. Be careful not to damage any of the fur. Snip open the stitches around the armholes. If you are going to use the sleeves, snip the stitches at the cuffs and at the armholes.

STEP 2: Remove the lining. Take out any canvas interlining there is in the coat. Depending on the type of fur, you will find some or a great many tiny overstitched seams on the inside of the fur. Mink coats, for instance, have hundreds of seams when "let out." It is a method of cutting the short skins of the mink diagonally, realigning them, and stitching them back together again to make a full-length coat without resorting to horizontal seams. This is part of the furrier's craft. Leopard does not have as many seams because the beauty of the leopard is in its natural markings.

STEP 3: Using a pencil or tailor's wax, mark the center of the leopard pattern (the backbone line) onto the wrong (skin) side. With a right-angled ruler, measure and mark your pillow shape. You will be slivering off the corners, which may give you a tiny bit more fur to play with. Every bit counts.

STEP 4: Cut the fur. Furriers cut with a sharp knife on the skin side so as not to sheer off any of the fur. I use a craft knife, a razor blade in a holder, or an X-acto knife. Some furs can be cut with scissors if you make sure the blade tucks underneath the fur as you cut so you don't damage surface hairs.

STEP 5: Lay your square (or in the pillow pictured, rectangle) of fur onto the ground fabric (in this case, dark brown brushed cowhide, or suede). Decide how much of this surround you want to show as a frame.

Left: **This pillow was made from an old needlepoint bellpull. The fringe is old, too, and was saved from a different project.**

Above: **Sitting on an armchair upholstered in antique fabric is a pillow inspired by a Lowestoft plate. (Lowestoft was the port where Chinese Export china arrived in England, hence the name.) On the nearby table are pieces of Lowestoft china.**

Left: **This is the first pillow I painted. The design is copied from the wallpaper in this country bedroom. The nineteenth-century belter chair is covered with an antique chintz that shows another variation of the birds and basket motif.**

STEP 6: At this point you will be able to decide the overall size of the pillow. Cut the suede, shaping off the corners as for a basic knife-edge pillow (see Diagram 6 on page 33).

STEP 7: Using the suede front as a pattern, cut the same shape in antique velvet. Notch the center bottom of both the suede and the velvet, deciding as you do which way you want the nap of the velvet pile to brush.

STEP 8: Shape the corners of the fur center very slightly. On the pillow in the photograph I cut $\frac{3}{8}$ inch (1 cm) off at the corners to nothing at a point $2\frac{1}{2}$ inches (6.5 cm) down the sides—so that it fitted onto the suede background frame. Check that the proportions look right on your pillow, then pin in place. If you find that pins don't readily go through the fur and suede, you can stick the fur in place with rubber cement or double-sided adhesive tape. Make sure the sticking elements are not at the very edges of the fur, or they will interfere with the machine stitching.

STEP 9: Using a size 16 machine needle, (for heavyweight fabrics), sew the fur directly onto the suede. Use a large stitch. Sueded leather tends to stick as you sew, so go slowly and pull it along if necessary. You may want to use a Teflon-coated foot.

STEP 10: Topstitch the braid by machine along its outside edge first. Start at one corner, allowing extra where you start for a seam. Match the thread exactly so the stitches will disappear into the braid. Make sure that the braid is the same distance from the edge of the pillow front all the way around.

STEP 11: Sew the braid along its inside edge. When doing so, miter the corners by simply folding the extra braid in a slanting line. If the braid is heavy, you may need to hand-stitch the mitered corners to flatten them. Press the braid if needed, or machine-topstitch along the slanting line.

STEP 12: Sew the cord on tape to the outside edge of the suede front of the pillow, using a zipper foot.

Stitch as close to the cording as possible, right in the groove between the cord and tape. Go slowly, notching the tape at the corners so it will lie flat. Allow 2 inches (5 cm) overlap of cord on tape. To join the cord as invisibly as possible, mark or notch the tape on both ends when you come to the bottom notch on the suede, and cut the tape allowing $\frac{1}{4}$-inch (7-mm) overlap on each end. Sew the ends of the tape together. Overlap the cords, weaving one into the other so that the join is as invisible as possible. You may have to secure the ends of the cord by hand. Machine-stitch over the ends taking one stitch at a time and lifting the foot occasionally because of the thickness. Try not to break the machine needle!

STEP 13: Lay the back and the front together, making sure the notches match and the pile runs the right way. Start sewing about 2 inches (5 cm) up on one side. Use the previous stitching as a guide and go $\frac{1}{16}$ inch (1.5 mm) farther in so you really get close to the cord. If not, the tape will show, spoiling the look of the pillow. I find it best to make a groove with my nail. The amount of difficulty depends on how fat the cord is. Stop stitching when you come 2 inches (5 cm) down on the last side, which leaves an opening for turning.

STEP 14: Turn right side out, examine the seam, and go over any places where the tape shows.

STEP 15: Make the pillow interior. If the pillow is not a standard size, you may be better off using bed pillows cut down to size.

STEP 16: Insert the pillow interior and stuff extra fluff in the corners if needed. With a leather needle and heavy buttonhole thread, ladder-stitch up the side. Fluff up pillow and make sure it is clean from all fur hairs.

PILLOW WITH BLAZER EMBLEM

What about recycling Father's worn-out blazer? The fabric may be moth-eaten, but the pocket insignia is still intact. Why not use it on a pillow for the den? You may find a wonderful antique emblem, or you might get one from his old school or from his club, such as the one on page 74.

Pick the trimmings to frame and embellish the pillow accordingly. Take the badge with you when you are looking for accompanying braids and lay them out in the store to make sure you select the ones that are the most flattering to the badge. You may find that a scarlet plaited braid is better looking than a braid of antiqued silver, for example. Perhaps two—or more—rows of a very narrow corded braid, like soutache, that pick up colors from the badge might be more complementary than a single flat braid.

Because badges are small, the pillow should not be a large one. Choose menswear colors such as black, navy, red, khaki, or gray, and select trimmings that have a masculine appearance.

MATERIALS

Blazer badge

½ yard (46 cm) of good-quality worsted flannel or gabardine or a leftover remnant

1 yard (1 m) of antiqued gold or silver braid ¾ inch to 1 inch (2 cm to 3 cm) wide to outline the badge

2 yards (1.8 m) of a narrow flat antiqued gold or silver braid (or braid of your choice) to sew on the pillow front as a frame, mitering the corners

2 yards (1.8 m) antiqued gold or silver 1½-inch (4-cm) metallic fringe (or fringe of your choice) to edge the pillow

Pillow interior: Because this is a masculine type of pillow, made of a sturdy fabric, it can be firm, of kapok rather than delicate down.

METHOD

STEP 1: Cut the back and front of a square pillow to the size of your pillow interior. Sliver off the corners and make a bottom notch as for a basic pillow (see Diagram 6 on page 33).

STEP 2: Pin the badge in place on the front, making sure it is slightly above center.

STEP 3: Sew the badge on with tiny hand stitches, or topstitch it by machine if it is on a piece of fabric.

STEP 4: Pin the wider flat braid in place to frame the insignia, starting at one of the bottom corners.

STEP 5: Topstitch the wider braid on by machine if it will be unnoticeable, or else by hand. Sew the outside edge of the braid first, then the inside, mitering the corners by folding the excess into a 45-degree slant.

STEP 6: Mark a line with pins 2 inches (5 cm) away from the braid frame. Pin the narrow braid on this line and topstitch it by machine.

STEP 7: Join the front of the pillow to the back, leaving an opening for turning. Turn the pillow right side out.

STEP 8: Sew the heading of the fringe by hand onto the edge of the front of the pillow, starting at the center bottom notch.

STEP 9: Stuff in the interior filler, make sure the corners have enough filling, and add more if needed. Ladder-stitch up the opening and dress down the pillow by plumping it in all directions.

PAINTED PILLOWS

In the nineteenth century it was fashionable for ladies to stencil what were called theorem paintings, usually depicting flowers and fruit. Though most were painted on paper to hang on walls, some were painted on velveteen. Keith bought a cushion years ago from Colefax & Fowler, the decorating firm where he worked as John Fowler's assistant. The cushion, to use the English term, was made from a sophisticated stenciled painting of a bunch of flowers—an iris, a carnation, and a tulip—in faded shades of blue and brown on a toast velveteen ground. The painting was framed in fine brown

A wonderful present for a man is a pillow made of good-quality menswear flannel with an embroidered blazer emblem on it, embellished with antiqued braid and fringe.

Right: This painted pillow on a cane and leather invalid chair commemorates our cat Mavis, and is based on a child's illustration.

Below: A pillow shown here was made of scraps from a discarded leopard-skin coat. To make the pillow larger, the fur was framed in dark brown sueded leather and backed with dark brown linen velvet. A Greek key ribbon outlines the fur, and a tricolor cord embellishes the perimeter of the pillow. The simpler pillow placed behind merely has a black piping.

cotton tape and set onto a brown silk satin self-piped cushion. We've never been able to tell if the painting is English or American (Mrs. Lancaster, John Fowler's partner, was American and may have brought this theorem painting from America). This elegant cushion, which we still enjoy, inspired me to try doing some painted pillows myself (see page 66).

First I experimented with acrylic paint, but I used it straight from the tube, which was too thick, and it sat on the surface of fabric like a hard blob. I discovered with time how to mix it with water to get a less lumpy effect, and how, by adding more water, to create more watercolorlike impressions. Once completely dry, acrylic paint is permanent.

The first pillow I painted was of a detail taken from an American wallpaper in a bedroom in our farmhouse in the country. It showed a stylized basket of fruit and flowers flanked by two birds. I painted it on a piece of slubbed silk, and framed the circular detail with dark green velvet (see Framed Pillow, page 65). The paint was mixed with just a tad too little water and some of the paint formed a hard crust on the surface of the silk. I discovered that if I added more water, the paintflowed into the silk too much. Therefore, silk was not exactly the ideal fabric to paint. However, I still use the pillow on a carved nineteenth-century bedroom chair even though the silk has begun to rot.

Next I tried painting on velveteen, and found the fabric easier to deal with. I painted a fantasy picture of our white cat sitting on a pile of books and gazing into a goldfish bowl. The inspiration was a simply drawn Edwardian child's illustration. I used toast-colored velveteen so that the white cat would show up adequately. The painting was edged with green velveteen piping to match a frog in the fish bowl, surrounded with pale rust-colored satin, and backed with deep rust velveteen.

Since then I have tried painting on silk taffeta and on smooth, tightly woven cotton, but I have come to the conclusion that velveteen is the best of all because it bestows a softness that has the authentic, traditional look of theorem paintings. But painting on velveteens—and the more luxurious, silkier velvet—is fairly unforgiving. You cannot erase, though you can paint lightly on top of a mistake. To transfer a design from a book or picture onto the velvet, make sparse marks with light gray paint, merely sketching in a few lines to get the proportions right, then start freehand in the center and work out from there.

To paint pillows, make sure that you have several sizes of good watercolor brushes. You must have the very best fine-tipped camel hair brush for the tiny details. You will also need a good palette for mixing paint, so that you can add varying amounts of water to get the right consistency for your purpose. I use a round metal palette circled with indentations for the paint. Try out paint on a scrap of fabric if you are unsure of the effect, rather the way you might when painting a watercolor.

Originally I placed the velveteen in an embroidery hoop to paint it, but now I find it just as easy to pin a piece of velveteen onto a drawing board. Pin the velvet so that the nap strokes downward, as this makes for a more natural way of making your brushstrokes.

I have never used stencils in pillow making (yet!), though I have seen many pretty stenciled pillows. Craft shops sell many varieties of stencil motifs, such as pineapples (a symbol of hospitality), eagles, and wreaths. You can also design and cut your own stencils.

Keep a cache of design ideas that can be used in painting pillows: flowers, fruit, birds, animals (especially favorite pets), garlands, folk art, classical details, decorative ribbon bows, interesting lettering, buildings, and drawings that amuse you. One of my favorite sources is the decorative illustrations of *Les Fleurs Animées* (1847) designed by Jean-Ignace Grandville. Other sources may be old magazines, such as the *Gazette du Bon Ton,* a chic little French fashion magazine published in the early part of this century with wonderful drawings. These and other inspirational publications can often be found in libraries with a good decorative or fashion art section.

Once the painting is complete, it can be framed in the same way as needlepoint, as seen in the photographs in this chapter. The same rules apply. Pick all the fabrics and trimmings to enhance the painting and bring out the best in it.

Since painting my first pillow, I have done many more, some for my family for fun or to commemorate certain events. I have given others as gifts to friends, even basing some pillows on photographs of people. For instance, for the fiftieth birthday of English artist Richard Smith, I painted a pillow based on a photograph taken by Lord Snowdon of him sitting on a hammock in his studio. As a play on the names of a couple called Buck and Pearl Dean, I painted the head of a stag with a pearly necklace for their fiftieth wedding anniversary. For a chocolate-manufacturing friend always referred to as the Easter Bunny—who was also Master of the Reading Hunt in Pennsylvania—I painted a rabbit in a hunting-pink riding habit blowing a tallyho on a hunting horn. Many years ago, for fashion designer Anne Fogarty, I painted a croquis of her, with her *tiny* waist, typically full skirt, and her two poodles.

If you want to give a present of a painted pillow, try to make it truly personal.

CHAPTER 6

SHAPED PILLOWS

Most pillows are square or oblong. This chapter describes more unusual pillows of various shapes and sizes.

Usually the need for a round, oval, or long thin pillow is determined by the shape of a piece of embroidery or lace that you want to incorporate in the design, or by the design on printed fabric. The simplest round or oval pillows are those with a plain knife edge. A simple piping can be trapped into the edge to fence in the design and add a shot of another color. In any case, the techniques for these shaped pillows are similar to those for making the square pillows described in the previous chapters.

Round, oval, square, and oblong pillows can be given extra height and dimension by the addition of gussets, thus making a round pillow drum-shaped, and a square pillow box-shaped. For a softer look, the gusseted sides of pillows can be ruched (gathered at both top and bottom).

A most unusual pillow is a spherical one that looks like a ball. Though it is suitable only in certain nontraditional settings, it can be very amusing to decorate with. I remember seeing three spherical pillows of slightly different sizes made of three shades of greenish gray velvet—all held in a sequence by a velvet rope. They were on a simple mouse-colored velvet sofa in a neo–art deco house in Seattle, designed by Jean Jongeward. It was the perfect setting for these extraordinary pillows.

Similarly, pillows can be pyramid-shaped as well as cube-shaped, with appliqués on the sides. A nursery would be a great setting for spherical, drum-shaped, pyramid-shaped, or cube-shaped pillows. The stuffings for these should be firm and washable. Sometimes the fabric design inspires an unusually shaped pillow. Eliptical or rhomboid-shaped pillows may be suggested by a printed chintz.

Cylindrical pillows are traditionally found at the ends of Regency sofas. They may be trimmed with passementerie, and perhaps have a tassel hanging down from the center of the end. In a far more casual setting, in a dining room of a Montana fishing ranch, I saw cylindrical pillows made from the legs of jeans, with the ends tied like Christmas crackers.

Heart-shaped pillows are perfect as presents on St. Valentine's Day. They can be lovely as small, white, lacy confections; sentimental in pink velvet; or dramatic in vivid red. When my daughter Emma was a teenager, she was given a huge red free-form satin heart pillow, fringed in black, sewn by her boyfriend. (I was most impressed!) A heart-shaped pillow is especially delightful if it has a personal message embroidered or painted on it.

There are a number of ways to make shaped pillows that fall into the category of playthings. For example, take a look at the many versions of animal-shaped pillows based on nineteenth- and early-twentieth-century toys: cats, pugs, rabbits, squirrels, ducks, toucans, fancy Kate Greenaway–style little girls, soldier boys—we've even got a Tommy (the slang name for an English infantryman) from the First World War! I have included in this chapter, just for fun, an angel pillow, one that would be at home on a bed.

A grouping of shaped pillows made from antique lace complements a Victorian bed.

Experiment and incorporate some of the techniques in the previous chapters to invent many original designs for yourself.

ROUND QUILTED PILLOW

I determined the size and shape of this pillow by the design of the quilting, which was a scrap saved from a vintage white-on-white bedcover. This beautiful hand-stitched piece of stylized flowers in circular motifs was badly worn but I hated to part with it and so created interesting pillows with the material. The quilt yielded several pillows, some round, some square. A tiny red piping decorates the edge of the round pillow in the photograph. The pillow has been very useful as a support for me when reading in bed. (The other smaller scraps became pot holders!) See the top-right photograph on page 83.

OVAL DOILY BOUDOIR PILLOW

I happened to be looking through some household linens that had been embroidered in the 1880s by my mother's great-aunts when I came across an oval-shaped doily that had seen better days. The hand-tatted border surrounded a center of fine white pinwale piqué, which had been embroidered around its edge with featherstitching. Since I was unable to remove a stain long ingrained in the piqué, I decided to cut the fabric away, leaving only enough to show the row of featherstitched embroidery. A narrow strip of lace machine-sewn on top of the piqué disguised the raw edge. An alternative would have been to turn the raw edge in and hem it with tiny stitches. As you can see from the photographs on pages 50 and 83 (middle right), nothing has been lost in the general effect of the pillow by eliminating the center of the doily.

METHOD

STEP 1: Since the doily dictated the size and shape of the pillow, I had to make the oval pillow form myself because it was not a standard shape or size. To cut a good oval I often draw around an oval serving dish or a large platter—a useful and speedy trick. I made the outside casing of the pillow of off-white glazed chintz that blended well with the tatted doily.

STEP 2: For piping, I used a heavy cream-colored ottoman that I chose because the color, though slightly darker, complemented the chintz and the tatting, which had slightly oxidized over the years. I also made this choice because the heavy rib of the ottoman would resemble a thick cord when made into bias piping.

You might prefer to edge a similar type of pillow with a frill of lace instead of piping. If so, gather the lace, as close to its edge as possible. Sew the gathered lace onto the front of the pillow leaving a $\frac{5}{8}$-inch (16-mm) space in from the raw edge. Use this stitch holding the lace as a guide when you stitch the front to the back on the wrong side, but take only a $\frac{1}{2}$-inch (13-mm) seam allowance so that you do not catch the lace in the seam.

STEP 3: Proceed as for the basic pillow (page 32).

ROUND RUCHED PILLOW

This type of pillow was popular in the 1920s and 1930s, when they were often made of crisp, solid silk taffeta. The only embellishment was generally a narrow self-piping between the circles and the side ruching. Pillows like this also work well in satin, cotton taffeta, glazed chintz, or, for a bedroom, dotted swiss (point d'esprit). Keep in mind that you cannot easily put a zipper in this type of pillow nor make a sham back, so try to pick a washable fabric if the pillow is to be light in color. I chose a white calendered cotton, which is a less stiff version of glazed chintz. I created the size of the circle on the top of the pillow (see the bottom-right photograph on page 83) to fit well with a white hand-crocheted doily 8 inches (20 cm) in diameter that I loved but had never used before. There is no reason why the top of the pillow could not be 10 inches or 11 inches (25 cm or 28 cm) across, and the ruching the same size or smaller. I surrounded the crocheted doily with a white moss fringe, a small piece left over from another project (the same fringe that is used for the angel's "hair" on page 83). You might choose a simple cotton fringe instead.

MATERIALS

1 yard (1 m) of pillow fabric
A circular crocheted doily
1 yard (1 m) of white moss, or similar fringe
½ yd (46 mm) of white cotton from drum-shaped pillow interior and stuffing of down or polyester fiberfill

METHOD

STEP 1: From the pillow fabric cut 2 circles the size of your doily, allowing ½ inch (13 mm) extra all around for seams. By folding the circles in half along the grain, and then in quarters, notch at the edge quarter circles on both pieces.

STEP 2: Make the interior of white cotton. This should be drum-shaped, 13 inches (33 cm) in diameter, with a 3-inch (8-cm) strip fold gusset, and stuffed with down or polyester fiberfill. Simply join the gusset strip around the edge of one of the circles taking a ½ inch (13 mm) seam, then join the second circle to the other edge of gusset, leaving an opening for turning.

STEP 3: Sew the fringe around the edge of the doily.

STEP 4: Measure the circumference of the circle. Cut a bias strip 9 inches (23 cm) wide and two and

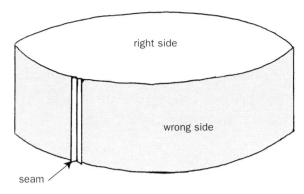

When making the interior form for the ruched pillow, cut a strip for a gusset 3 inches (8 cm) wide and long enough to go around the edges of the top and bottom circles. Join the ends of the gusset, taking ½-inch (13-mm) seams.

a half times as long as this measurement. You will probably have to make some joining seams on the bias, as for narrow bias strips. Make all necessary seams and press them open.

STEP 5: Notch and mark with pins at the half and quarter points of the strip to use as a guide when fitting the gathered strip to the circle. As with ruffles, if you make a notch only it will get lost in the gathers, whereas a pin will show. Gather both sides of the strip.

STEP 6: Match the pins on the gathered bias strip to the notches on the wrong side of the circles. Pin into place and stitch the front carefully, not catching the fringe or the edge of the doily in the stitches.

STEP 7: Repeat at the back, but leave a large enough opening to fit in the pillow form.

STEP 8: Turn the pillow right side out.

STEP 9: Stuff in the pillow form, making sure the gathers are even and that the pillow interior is well placed inside the casing. Use a ladder stitch to close the opening.

CYLINDRICAL PILLOWS

To cut a simple cylindrical pillow, use the same principle as for the previous drum-shaped pillow, but alter the proportions. Determine the length you need for the pillow (for example, if it is for a sofa end, measure the horizontal platform of the seat) and the diameter of the rounded ends. Decide if the end of the pillow should have self-piping, contrast piping, or no piping at all, and cut accordingly.

If you wish to make a gathered end with a tassel coming from the center (as in the photograph on page 47), cut a rectangular piece of fabric the length of the circumference of the end circle by the radius of the circle, and add seam allowances. Sew the ends of this piece together and press.

Gather *tightly* along one side. Tassels for this purpose often have a rosette from which the tassel protrudes. This can be hand-sewn in place to hide the point where the gathers converge. Otherwise you can trap the loop on the end of the tassel in the gathers, pulling them up into one clump. Where the gathers converge is a place where you may want to add a rosette or a *macaron*. Finish off by hand on the wrong side. Sew the ungathered side into the end of the cylinder. Leave the opening to turn a cylindrical pillow along the side of the cylinder.

If you prefer, you can make a simple circular end to the cylinder. Keith designed a showhouse sofa with a slipcover made of striped ticking. He created very effective ends simply from a circle of mitered stripes.

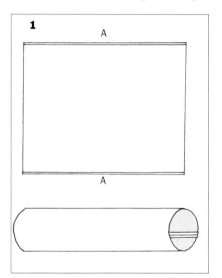

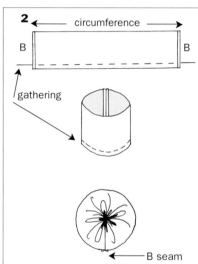

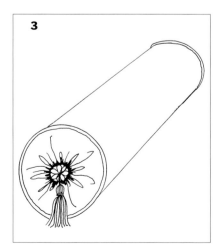

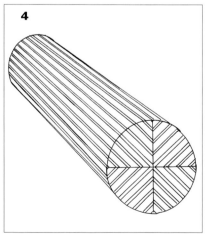

1. To cover a cylindrical pillow form, cut a rectangle for the tubular part of the pillow the length required by the circumference of the tube required and add ½-inch (13-mm) seam allowances all around. Seam the length of the fabric to form a tube (A seam to A seam) leaving an opening for turning later, and press seam open.

2. If the pillow is to have end pieces with gathering in the centers, cut 2 rectangles the circumference of the tube by the radius of the round ends, plus ½-inch (13-mm) seam allowances all around. Seam the shorter sides (B seam to B seam) to form small tubes and press open. Gather one side of each tube tightly to form circles.

3. Finish with rosettes, or *macarons,* sewn on by hand or set tassels into the centers by hand. Add piping around the circumferences, if desired. On the wrong side sew the gathered circles into either end of the tubular pillow. Turn through the opening left on the side of the tube, stuff in the pillow form. Ladder-stitch to close.

4. A way to arrange stripes at the end of a cylindrical pillow.

Right: This round boudoir pillow was suggested by the circular white-on-white quilted design on a vintage bedcover. All it needed in the way of embellishment was a simple contrasting piping.

Above: An oval-shaped doily made by my great-aunts inspired this oval boudoir pillow.

Below: A combination of lace scraps can be assembled to make an angel pillow for a bed.

Above: A delicate embroidered and lace-edge doily was threaded with a satin ribbon and centered on a round pillow.

Above: This round pillow, embellished with a crocheted doily edged with moss fringe, has been given height by its ruched sides.

FLOOR PILLOWS

Large, firm pillows can make wonderful hassocks on the floor. An amusing idea is to sew two large, square, well-stuffed cushions one on top of the other, held by a big, self-covered button on top and at the bottom. You will need the longest, strongest upholstery needle, and doubled heavy thread. To wax the thread and make it even stronger, draw it tightly against a candle. (Ribbed wax for thread, like emery pincushions for de-rusting needles, used to be a staple in every nineteenth-century workbox.) Arrange one pillow straight and the other on the diagonal.

HEART-SHAPED PILLOWS

To make a pattern, fold a piece of paper in half, draw half the heart, then cut it and open the fold. Remember to allow ½-inch (13-mm) turnings all around. Heart-shaped pillows are usually completely decorative, so they can be embellished with lace, ribbon, beads—you name it!

LONG, THIN CUSHIONS

Some embroidery, especially needlepoint, was designed in long, thin pieces, probably intended for a foot stool in front of a fire. These pieces can be made up into elegant pillows to be placed along the back of a sofa in the style of the Duchess of Windsor.

SPHERICAL PILLOWS

Spherical pillows are not to everyone's taste, but in certain settings they work well as decorative accents. Using simple geometry, you can work out a pattern for an eight-sectioned pillow similar in appearance to a beach ball. I find it most effective to use a soccer ball as a form and cut muslin pieces to fit it exactly, as shown in the ball diagram on the facing page. After you have made the perfect section as a pattern, cut it in paper with ½-inch (13-mm) turnings added. Then make up the ball in muslin, leaving one section open to turn, and use this not only to check your pattern but also as the interior form to fill with down or fiberfill. The sections can be cut all of the same fabric, or for fun, in two different colors alternating the sections, or even in eight different colors. When the pillow is cut and stitched in your selected fabric, sew a self-covered button where the seams converge.

ANGEL-SHAPED PILLOW

There is often a fine line between a stuffed toy and a pillow. This angel probably oversteps that line because it is not strictly speaking a pillow, but a limbless doll that looks very sweet on a bed. In the angel pictured on pages 82–83, I used many different fabrics and laces but only because they were small pieces left over from previous projects. There follows a list and description of each element, any one of which could be replaced by something similar. The laces used for the underskirt, dress neck, and mobcap may be all the same lace.

MATERIALS

A flounce (fabric with an embroidered edge) of white piqué with a deep eyelet embroidered border and a blue satin ribbon slotted through the eyelets. This flounce is to be the angel's dress and will dictate the design and size of the pillow. Plain fabric will suffice as a substitute, to which you may add a strip of lace or embroidery.

White velveteen for the angel's body and wings: ½ yard (46 cm)

White batiste for an underskirt: ½ yard (46 cm)

Narrow white lace to edge the underskirt: 2 yards (2 m)

Narrow white lace for the neck of the dress: ¼ yard (23 cm)

Elastic for the top of the dress: ¼ inch (7 mm) wide by ¼ yard (23 cm)

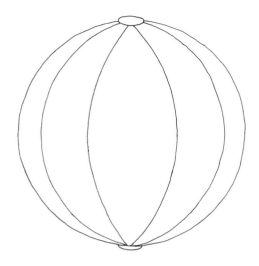

Use a soccer ball to make a pattern similar to a beach ball in eight even sections. First draw on the ball in pencil and then pin on muslin to make a pattern.

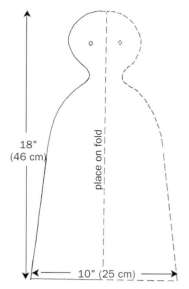

Make a pattern for the body of the angel in paper, and cut from white velveteen.

MATERIALS *(continued)*

White dotted swiss for the mobcap: about 16 inches (41 cm) square

White lace for the edge of the mobcap: 1 yard (1 m)

White moss fringe for hair: ¹⁄₂ yard (46 cm)

Small white lace doily for the halo, starched very stiff

White guipure lace to be sewn to the wings to resemble feathers: about ¹⁄₂ yard (46 cm)

2 small mother-of-pearl buttons for the eyes and contrasting thread

Stuffing for the body: fiberfill, kapok, or fluff from the dryer

Flannel or sheet fiberfill to sew inside the wings: ¹⁄₂ yard (46 cm). You might want some down to make them puff up.

Buckram interlining to go into the wings to keep them firm: ¹⁄₄ yard (23 cm)

Tiny beads for the necklace

BODY

METHOD

STEP 1: Cut the body shape as given in the below diagram from white velveteen with the pile going down.

STEP 2: Sew up the body, leaving the bottom open. Notch the seam allowance around the neck area so that the seams will open and lie flat when stuffed.

STEP 3: Turn right side out.

STEP 4: Stuff the body firmly using kapok or fiberfill or some other firm stuffing rather than down. I used fluff from the drying machine.

STEP 5: Sew up the bottom by hand. As this angel will be lying down, there is no need to make a standing base.

STEP 6: Sew 2 mother-of-pearl buttons on for eyes, using a contrasting thread. The thread pictured is periwinkle blue, sewn in a crisscross. Push the needle right through to the back of the head so that each button is slightly pulled into the head. Wind white thread several times around the neck to give it definition and knot firmly. With a pin, smooth out any wrinkles that may have formed. An alternative is to paint the angel's face using acrylic paint, watered down to give a soft effect.

STEP 7: If you have any tiny beads, string them around the neck as a necklace.

WINGS

METHOD

STEP 1: Cut the wings, shown in the diagram, double from velveteen and also from buckram interlining and either flannel or sheet fiberfill.

STEP 2: Sew around the wings on the wrong side, trapping the flannel or fiberfill and the buckram interlining all in the same stitch inside. Leave an opening at the bottom center.

STEP 3: Turn the wings right side out.

STEP 4: Stuff them with more fiberfill, or with down so that they puff up. Ladder-stitch the opening.

STEP 5: Sew guipure lace on by machine or hand, stitching through and through along the stalks and branches. Leave some parts of the lace unstitched to give a three-dimensional effect.

DRESS

STEP 1: Measure from the neck to 1 inch (25 mm) below the base. This is to establish the length to cut the dress. If the fabric has a finished embroidered bottom like the one shown, merely add 1 inch (25 mm) for the neck hem. If it is unfinished, add an extra ½ inch (13 mm) for a hem at the bottom, to which you will add an edging of lace. If the dress is to be 14 inches (35 cm) long, cut the fabric at least 30 inches (76 cm) wide.

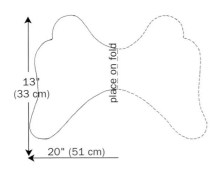

13" (33 cm)

place on fold

20" (51 cm)

Make a pattern as shown and cut the wings from white velveteen.

STEP 2: Sew a French seam at the back of the dress to form a cylinder. A French seam is done by making a tiny seam on the right side of the cloth, turning it to the wrong side, and making a slightly bigger seam. This way the seam is clean on both sides (diagrams 1 and 2 on the facing page).

STEP 3: Cut the batiste underskirt the same size. Make a French seam on the underskirt. Hem the bottom of the underskirt. Add an edging of lace to the underskirt.

STEP 4: Sew the top of the underskirt to the top of the dress. Topstitch a piece of lace ¾ inch (2 cm) in from the edge at the neck of the dress.

STEP 5: Press and stitch a hem at the neck ⅜ inch (1 cm) onto the wrong side, leaving ½ inch (13 mm) unstitched to insert the elastic. Using a safety pin at one end, slot the elastic through the neck hem and pull it to gather the top.

STEP 6: Place the dress over the head, round the neck, and finish off the elastic by hand so that it fits snugly. If you do not have elastic, a narrow ribbon or cord will do just as well.

MOBCAP

METHOD

STEP 1: Cut a circle to make the mobcap, 14 inches (35 cm) in diameter.

STEP 2: Single-hem the edge and sew on a lace edging.

STEP 3: Gather 1 inch (3 cm) in from the edge, using the largest machine stitch and pushing with the tip of your scissors.

STEP 4: Measure moss fringe to the size of the angel's head. Sew the fringe onto the line of gathering stitches on the mobcap, pinning it first to make sure the gathering fits to the fringe. Overlap and hand-stitch the ends of the fringe to prevent it from unraveling.

STEP 5: Place the mobcap on the angel's head with the seams of the moss fringe at the back and secure it with a couple of tiny hidden basting stitches.

STEP 6: Starch and press the doily so that it is really stiff. Stitch it by hand to the back of the angel's head so that it looks like a halo.

STEP 7: Sew the wings to the back of the angel by hand, stitching all the way through the dress to the body for firmness.

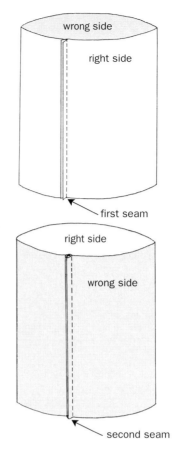

1. To make a French seam for the back of the angel's dress, make a seam less than 1/4 inch (7 mm) wide on the right side of the fabric. Press seam and turn to wrong side. **2.** Sew a fractionally bigger seam on the *wrong* side, trapping the raw edges inside.

CHAPTER 7

EAT PADS

From the days of ancient Greece and Rome up to today, hard benches, stools, and chairs have been made more comfortable by the addition of seat padding. Nowadays we demand the look of comfort in our rooms. Upholstered sofas and armchairs have become part of our interior landscape. Most of these upholstered pieces have thick, flat, loose pads that in America are usually called cushions. Many upright chairs with hard seats are upholstered, such as chairs that go around a formal dining room table. If they are not upholstered, removable, tied-on seat pads make them comfortable and inviting. In England this kind of seat pad is sometimes called a squab.

In the summer, easy-to-launder, flat cotton seat pads make metal chairs around an outdoor table casually comfortable. In our family we have collected chairs based on the style of those found in French parks, which are sometimes called "Parc Monceau" chairs. These chairs have punched metal seats and originally were designed as folding chairs, but age and layers of paint over the years have taken this advantage away. Our Parc Monceau chairs that are used outside are painted charcoal gray, and on them are dark green duck seat pads with white piping. Inside, on a porch around the table where we usually eat, the same Parc Monceau chairs are painted white and the seat pads, currently, are tiny green and white stripes.

Colored seat pads on chairs used outdoors or in a sunny room in the summer will fade sooner or later, so you have to either re-cover the pad every few years or make new ones. Using white or natural is a lovely idea, but difficult to keep looking spotlessly clean.

Seat pads on chairs are usually held in place with ties that fasten around upright at the back of the chair. These ties can be narrow or wide strips made from the same fabric as the seat pad, or they can be pieces of contrasting fabric, braid, or ribbon. When upright chairs are of good quality and of dark wood, the ties may be made of brown tape ¼ inch to ½ inch (7 mm to 13 mm) wide to blend with the wood and be as indiscernible as possible.

Some seat pads, rather than being flat as a pancake, are stuffed with polyester fiberfill and then tufted with four spaced, self-covered buttons sewn through the pad to hold the stuffing in place. More sophisticated seat pads use firm kapok wadding, and more buttons to hold the squab flat.

Wicker armchairs and sofas need a thick seat pad or heavy cushions rather than just throw pillows. On our white-painted wicker furniture we have a fern print designed by Suzanne Fontan that has survived the rigors of family life for nearly a quarter of a century, though the green piping has faded and repairs have been made. There are several classic fern prints available in the decorative textile markets, one in

Fabric-covered pads such as this one made of heavy furnishing moiré soften and protect chair seats. Five self-covered buttons on the top and on the bottom hold the padding in place. The brown tape ties that hold the pad in place are fastened around the shanks of the two back buttons underneath the pad.

particular a classic that was used by the innovative decorator Lady Mendel (Elsie de Wolfe).

Chairs with cane seats indubitably require seat padding. Caning tends to dry out in our centrally heated houses. Eventually cane becomes fragile, so using a seat pad is good protection.

A classic way to protect chairs that have caned backs is to attach a shaped back pad. This can be held in place by cord, thread, or narrow tape that can pass through the caning. A shaped back pad is often called by the French term *lambrequin,* which is a stiffened shaped piece of material (it can be of fabric, wood, or tin for decorative uses other than pillow making) that dips downward at the sides to form a somewhat proscenium-like effect to crown a curtain or bed hanging, as well as a chairback.

The stuffing in a seat pad or lambrequin can be cotton wadding, fiberfill in sheets, kapok, or even layers of brushed cotton flannel. Feathers and down are too soft and precious for seat pads. On a window seat, banquette, or outdoor sofa, it may be more suitable to use a 4-inch-thick (10-cm) seat pad of lightweight foam rubber cut to size.

KNIFE-EDGED PIPED SEAT PAD

MATERIALS

Brown wrapping paper for making a pattern
Filling: cotton wadding, sheets of fiberfill, or layers of flannel
Fabric: 1 yard (1 m) is enough
Piping fabric: ½ yard (46 cm)
Piping filler cord: 2 yards (1.8 m)
Matching thread
Chair for which seat pad is intended

METHOD

STEP 1: To make a template or pattern of the seat of the chair, cut brown paper a little bigger than the chair seat. Lay the paper on the seat and use a pencil to mark the shape you wish the seat pad to be.

Make sure you follow the shape of the seat where the uprights set into the back of the seat. Make notches where the ties should be inserted. Likewise, if the front has arms, follow the seat shape around where the arms are set. The seat pad will look best if you make it cover the caning entirely but allow some of the wood frame to show. The late John Fowler of Colefax & Fowler always said to allow ½ inch (13 mm) of the wood to show at the front and sides but to take the pad all the way to the back of the seat.

STEP 2: To check that the template is symmetrical, fold the paper pattern through the center and make any necessary corrections.

STEP 3: Mark the fabric. When you lay the paper pattern onto the fabric, make sure you lay the center fold of the pattern along the center of the fabric design. This is important in any patterned fabric, stripes and checks as well as prints. Allow a ⅝-inch (16-mm) seam allowance all around the pattern. Beginners may prefer to cut a perfect pattern that includes seam allowances. A seam allowance of ⅝ inch (16 mm) will give you ½-inch (13-mm) seams plus a little extra to account for the rising thickness of the pad.

STEP 4: Cut a top and a bottom piece from fabric. Notch in all the right angles or deeply curved areas.

STEP 5: Cut the filling to the pattern size minus the seam allowances.

STEP 6: Cut strips for the ties. For simple, narrow machine-stitched ties, cut 4 strips 2 inches (5 cm) by 7 inches (18 cm). These measurements will make 6 inch (16 cm) long ties just under ½ inch (3 cm) wide. If you prefer longer ties, cut the desired length plus 1 inch for seam allowance, and four times the desired finished width.

STEP 7 : Press in ¼-inch (7-mm) seams all around the tie strips, then press the strips in half lengthwise, as shown in the following diagram.

To make simple, machine-stitched ties for seat pads: Cut strips and press in the seams; fold the strips in half lengthwise; and topstitch around the edges.

STEP 8 : Topstitch all around the edges of the folded ties.

STEP 9: From the piping fabric, cut enough bias piping strips to go around the outside edge of the seat pad. Join the piping strips and press the seams open. Encase the piping cord into the bias strip and sew using a zipper foot. (See Step 4, page 33.) Sew the piping to top of the seat pad fabric using a zipper foot and starting at the center back. Join the piping on the bias at the center back of the pad as shown in Diagrams 12 through 17 on page 35. Notch the piping at corners and curves where necessary so it will lie flat.

STEP 10: Join the top of the pad to the bottom. At the back corners, trap in the ties at the appropriate places. Leave an opening along the back of the seat pad through which to turn the pad cover right side out.

STEP 11: Turn the cover right side out, and the ties will automatically come out.

STEP 12: Set in the filling, smoothing it out and making sure it is flat inside the pad cover. Hand-sew the back of seat pad closed with a ladder-stitch.

If the seat pad has to be washed frequently, you can put a zipper in the back between the piping and bottom of casing so that the padding can be removed. The padding should be covered in some form of sheeting so that it can slide in and out of the casing easily. Don't use zippers on pads that are made of formal fabrics or pads on antique chairs.

STEP 13: Place the pad on the chair and tie the ties in either a small bow or a simple reef knot.

WIDE TIES

Though I personally prefer simple ties, you may prefer wide self-fabric ties to be fastened in bows at the back of the seat pads to give a dressier appearance. Depending on the weight of the fabric selected, these ties can be made in single fabric with a tiny machined hem around the edges, or the fabric can be doubled, which will give a clean finish on all sides. (See Diagram 5 on page 95.)

Ties should be 3 inches (8 cm) wide when finished. Each end (of 4 per seat pad) should be 20 inches (51 cm) long to make a generous bow with ends hanging down at least 10 inches (25 cm); you may want to make the ends even longer. Slant the ends of the ties so that they resemble cut ribbons.

SEAT PADS WITH SIDE GUSSETS

Some seats require more thickness than a knife edge. For these seat pads, a separate gusset has to be set in all around the pad. (See the diagrams on page 95.) Gussets can range from 1 inch (3 cm) wide to as much as 4 inches (10 cm) wide for a wicker sofa pad or a banquette. For thickness less than 1 inch (3 cm), a gusset is generally unnecessary.

METHOD

STEP 1: For a gusset, cut a piece of fabric the length of the outside circumference of the seat pad by the height needed for the gusset insert, plus $\frac{1}{2}$ inch (13 mm) on all sides for seam allowances. When cutting the fabric, make sure that the center front of the gusset matches—or continues—the design of the center front of the top of the seat pad.

Right: On this painted Regency chair, the seat pad is made of heavy red silk-faced satin, with brown ottoman piping. Unobtrusive brown tape ties hold the chair pad in place at the back.

Below: This French fern print was designed by Suzanne Fontan in the 1930s. Prints like this work well as seat pads and pillows on vintage wicker furniture, and even on this simple, rustic child's chair.

This cane-seated and cane-backed chair has been given a flat seat pad and a matching lambre-quin-shaped pad for the back. The pads are made of a linen print and edged with red piping.

If you have to make seams in the gusset, make sure that these match also.

STEP 2: The filling must be firm, of the same thickness as the gusset, and cut as closely as possible to the dimensions of the seat pad cover minus seam allowances.

STEP 3: Twice as much piping or cording will be needed for a seat pad with a gusset than for a knife-edged pad. Sew the piping to the top of the seat pad and also to the bottom.

STEP 4: Sew the gusset between the top and the bottom of the pad. Leave a space for turning at the bottom back of the seat pad cover.

STEP 5: Turn the pad right side out.

STEP 6: Stuff in the pad interior and sew up the opening by hand.

ZIPPERS IN SEAT PADS

If a zipper is to be used—and I don't advise it if the chairback will show—the gusset has to be cut somewhat differently.

METHOD

STEP 1: Make vertical seams in the gusset where it reaches the side back corners, and allow ½-inch (13-mm) turnings.

STEP 2: Across the back, cut the gusset in 2 horizontal pieces. A ¾-inch (2-cm) seam should be allowed to set the zipper in. Regular ½-inch (13-mm) seams should be allowed on the bottom and

top of the gusset. The zipper will be set between these 2 pieces. On all these seams, pay attention to matching the design of the fabric.

STEP 3: Set the zipper in first, using the zipper foot. Then join the gusset into one piece, and proceed as above. Because of the zipper, you do not have to leave an opening to turn the pillow right side out.

Ties, if narrow, are best set between the bottom of the pad and the gusset. Ties can be made the width of the side gusset and long enough to be tied in large bows. If you prefer this look, the gusset should be cut with side back seams as for the zipper, and the ties should be set in vertically.

RUCHED GUSSETS

The side gusset can be ruched as a variation. For this the gusset should be cut twice as long as the outside edge of the seat pad, and gathered on both sides prior to setting in. Sometimes only slight ruching is called for, in which case the gusset need be only 3 inches (8 cm) longer and eased rather than gathered into the top and bottom of the pad.

FRAMED SEAT PADS

You may want to set a piece of needlepoint onto a seat pad. Follow the technique for a Framed Pillow (page 65). Bear in mind that the piping or cording outlining the needlepoint should not be too thick because it will be on the surface of the seat pad, and a fat cord will be uncomfortable to sit on.

Once you have framed the needlepoint for the top of the pad, proceed as for a regular seat pad.

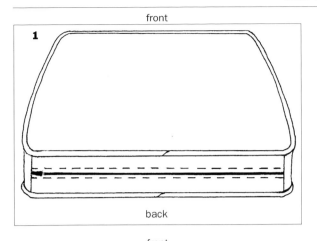

front

1

back

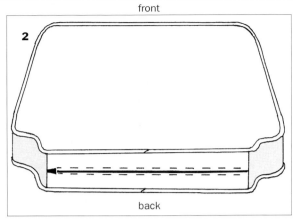

front

2

back

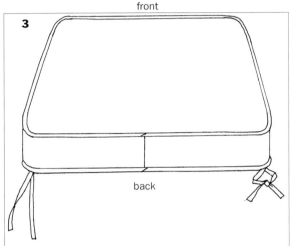

front

3

back

front

4

back

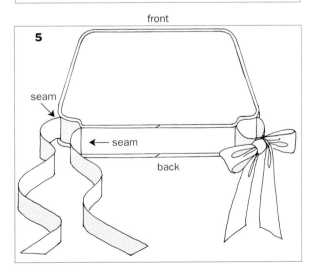

front

5

seam

← seam

back

1. To set a zipper in the back of a seat pad with a gusset, make vertical seams at the back corners of the gusset. Cut the back of the gusset in 2 horizontal pieces, allowing ¾ inch (2 cm) with which to set in the zipper.

2. If the back of the seat pad is shaped to accommodate chair-back uprights, set zipper across the narrowest part of the back between the cut-away corners.

3. On a seat back with a gusset, set small ties together on the bottom seam, the one closest to the actual seat.

4. If the seat pad has been cut away at the back corners to accommodate chair uprights, set one tie on the back and one tie on the side as shown, repeating with 2 more ties on the other back corner.

5. For wide ties, make vertical seams in the back of the gusset to set the ties in. Set both ties into one seam if the pad has a simple back with no shaping. If the pad has been cut away for chair uprights, make 2 seams at each rear corner at the outside edges of the shape that has been cut away in which to set the ties. If you want the ties to be wider than the gusset, fold a pleat in the ties as you set them in.

This window seat has been given a long cushion made of foam rubber covered in checked fabric and piped in red. Patchwork cushions add extra comfort.

LAMBREQUINS

The lambrequin on the back of a cane-backed chair should be of the same fabric as the seat pad. If there is a design on the fabric, the placement of it on the lambrequin should relate to its placement on the seat pad. If you have chosen an elaborate, pictorial design, you may want to use one part on the seat and another on the lambrequin. The design on the fabric may also dictate the shape of the lambrequin.

METHOD

STEP 1: Make a template or pattern for the lambrequin from paper, bearing in mind all the above. Check that the paper pattern is symmetrical by folding it through the center vertically. Add seam allowances. If the shaping of the lambrequin is very elaborate, involving sharp points or tight curves, you may be better off allowing only ¼-inch (7-mm) seam allowances to make the pad smoother when turned right side out. Notch the seams where there are curves and angles.

STEP 2: Cut the back and the front of the lambrequin.

STEP 3: Cut and make the piping, and if necessary, trim the seams to ¼ inch (7 mm) also to match the seams you have allowed on the lambrequin.

STEP 4: Outline the front of the lambrequin with piping.

STEP 5: Sew the back to the front, leaving an opening on one side for turning.

STEP 6: Turn the cover right side out. Poke the angles out gently with a knitting needle or the end of closed scissors.

STEP 7: Cut thin filling to the pattern shape. Insert the filling and smooth out. Sew up the seam with a ladder stitch, and press if necessary.

STEP 8: To attach the lambrequin to the cane-backed seat, hold it in place and mark two dots from the back, through the cane, where the lambrequin should be held. Some lambrequins are held in place simply by quadrupled thread, tied through the cane. I am always a little nervous that this will eventually cut through the cane, so I prefer to use very narrow ribbon or tape of a suitable color. One can always hand-dye inexpensive cotton tape. Sew this on just below the dots; gravity will always make the lambrequin slip downward slightly. Tie the tape in a small bow or a simple knot so that if the back of the chair shows, it won't look unsightly.

BANQUETTE AND WINDOW SEAT PADS

To make a large cushion for a window seat or banquette, the same principle is used as for a gusseted seat pad. The only real difference is the scale of the job.

Foam rubber is the easiest, most inexpensive, and most readily available interior to use. It is also light to move around. Foam rubber can be found in upholstery supply shops and stores that specialize in such products. There are different qualities and thicknesses from which to choose, and most places will cut the exact shape you want. If not, foam rubber can be cut easily with a sharp serrated knife or an electric carving knife.

For a banquette, you might prefer a slightly rounded edge to the cushion. You can trim off the edge using regular shears. To smooth any irregularities, and make the pad easier to slide into the outer casing, cover the foam rubber with plain muslin.

METHOD

STEP 1: If you use a printed design, decide if you want to run the fabric along the banquette in one piece (called railroading) or down the banquette the orthodox way so that the print faces you. If you cut it the orthodox way, the fabric will have to be seamed, so make sure all the seams match. The design on the gusset, too, should relate to the top (platform) of the cushion. Lay the fabric on the foam form and take your time about deciding this. Cutting fabric for the banquette will probably take longer than stitching it because, apart from the larger amount of fabric involved, it is similar to making a gusseted seat pad. Make sure the most important part of the design is centered on the banquette.

STEP 2: Decide if you want to use piping, and if so, whether it should be self-fabric, or a solid color picked out from the print, or a ready-made piping, or a cord on tape. Whether the cushion cover will be frequently washed or cleaned may influence the decision. For piping you will need to cut the length and the width of the cushion times four.

STEP 3: If the banquette is long and you wish to insert a zipper, follow the instructions for Zippers in Seat Pads on pages 94–95 but use two heavy upholstery zippers that meet in the center back of the gusset.

STEP 4: Proceed as for a gusseted seat pad.

CHAPTER 8

PILLOW ARRANGEMENT IN ROOM SETTINGS

Just having a good-looking pillow is not enough to make your room visually interesting. You should try a number of ways to place the pillow so that the room looks its best, for enhancing the room is one of the main reasons for making a pillow.

A professional decorator considers many requirements when designing a room: the flow of surrounding rooms leading into the space; the size and use of the room; the architectural details; what needs to go on the walls; what should go on the floor; the way the lighting works; how the windows should look; the arrangement of the furniture; how that furniture should be covered; and finally the details—the accessories. Pillows tossed on the furniture fall into this last category. When a decorator puts together a scheme, all these elements are brought together. Materials play a big part in the scheme—materials for upholstery and curtains, as well as carpeting. Using pillows allows the decorator to fine-tune the arrangement, emphasizing one color on a pillow here, introducing another color there, blending several colors on another pillow.

Decorators go to various sources to select swatches to show their clients, including the decorative fabric houses. In presenting the scheme, they will describe how many pillows will be required in the room with, say, a sofa, two upholstered armchairs, a slipper chair, and so forth. Some people like lots of pillows, others prefer fewer—but a sofa with no pillows on it at all can look mighty lonely!

TIPS ON ARRANGING PILLOWS

Many living rooms consist of a sofa with tables at either end holding lamps, one or two matching or different upholstered armchairs, a coffee table, plus some movable "draw up" furniture.

Depending on the sofa fabric, an appropriate way to organize pillows to go on it might be this:

• two large, down-stuffed, solid silk taffeta ones at the outer edges—as background for the other pillows
• two slightly smaller chintz or patterned pillows in a print used elsewhere in the room
• a precious, special needlepoint pillow in the center, maybe beaded, but of great quality
• to break the symmetry, another smaller embroidered, printed, or shaped pillow on and to one side of the backrest of the sofa.

An armchair usually has one pillow, but can have several, as does the child's chair with four tiny pillows pictured on page 62. Banquettes usually have one long cushion, but they are made more inviting by having several throw pillows as well. (See the toile banquette on page 16, the Regency flanged and cylindrical pillows on pages 20–21, and the window seat on page 96).

Don't be afraid of having *lots* of pillows on a sofa or daybed to make a statement and serve as a gallery, so to speak, for a collection of precious

Above: This sofa covered in a simple brown-and-white vermicelli print serves as a background for a variety of pillows. At the arms are leopard pillows and small but different size ocelot-printed pillows piped in red. A large red satin pillow with black moss fringe is balanced by a red seaweed-printed pillow with fan edging. A blue and silver beaded pillow depicting angels has a counter-part with a blue and white chintz pillow. A large beaded floral pillow framed in toast-colored ottoman with a blue wool moss fringe is flanked by two petit point pillows showing Arabian scenes. In the front is a tiny antique crocheted pillow puffed with red silk. Along the sofa back (in the style of the Duchess of Windsor) a long red pillow with black and white beading sits next to a grotesque mask painted on blue plush. They are flanked by two Victorian needlepoint pillows.

Right: Here is one of Irvine & Fleming's schemes for a sitting room. The drawing indicates sisal carpeting, a patterned rug, the placement of furniture, swatches for upholstery and curtains, and details of fabric and trimming for the pillows.

Right: A bentwood chair in a garden room/library gets a fat, zippered seat pad that is shaped around the front arms and the back uprights, and a fan-edged pillow covered in the same printed chintz as the curtains. An extra pillow of fine mitered stripes has a corded edge.

needlepoint. As seen in the photographs on pages 20–21 and 100, both pieces of furniture are loaded with pillows, leaving little room for a person to sit. However, many of us put some pillows aside when we sit, or use them to prop up a book, or for support. Pillows are, after all, meant to be movable objects.

Try to use an *idea* of symmetry as you place the pillows, but do not be slavish to it. Pillows should look as if they were accumulated over a period of time, rather than being too self-consciously placed there, brand new for this year's scheme. Allow some whimsy to creep in. Make some pillows of the same fabric but vary the size; or make pillows the same size, but vary the color or texture. Introduce a bit of shock—a bright unexpected color, or an amusing subject painted or embroidered on a pil-

low. Play with the arrangement from time to time. There are people who, having employed a decorator, take photographs to make absolutely sure the pillows get back to exactly the right places. The design scheme may well be the best arrangement, but try other groupings too as you add your own new pillows. Keep your rooms and your furnishings personal and special.

PLUMPING PILLOWS

No matter how beautiful the pillow, it will not look its best if it is not plumped up properly. It is depressing in the morning to enter a room with sagging pillows, so get into the habit of puffing them up when you retire at night. Plump a pillow horizontally and vertically to separate and distribute the down evenly. Some people put pillows in the dryer on the "fluff" cycle, but make sure your pillow is not too delicate for this treatment.

I personally don't like to see a pillow given a sharp karate chop that gives an exaggerated dip in the middle, but there are people who love their pillows to look that way.

If a pillow can be used front or back, up or down, vary these positions frequently. One-way, one-sided pillows tend to sag around the front at the bottom, and eventually the fabric there wears away, especially if it is silk. However, hang on to a favorite old pillow as long as you can. Some of the most successful rooms I've seen have had pillows in a state of "pleasing decay," as John Fowler used to say, with a patina of age and a few threadbare places. Don't despise them, but instead treat them gently as the fabulous invalids they are.

Taking a tip from the professional interior decorators, it is best to decide which room needs pillows and then determine specific colors and fabrics. Is the room to have a formal feeling? If so, are you searching for a luxurious heavy satin, or a soft and tactile velvet or chenille, or a cheerful floral chintz? In contrast, perhaps you need something bright and washable for a child's room. Maybe you want to find some cream velveteen on which to paint a personal pillow for a friend? Or you may be looking for some textile idea that excites you—a scrap of antique lace, a piece of precious real fur, fanciful passementerie, or a mixture of fabrics to make into a patchwork pillow.

Once you have determined the ambience you are after, searching for the fabrics you would like for your pillows becomes easier because you have a direction. Then, deciding the trimming, the size, and the placing of the pillows can be done in a logical progression. By focusing your ideas, and keeping within a general scheme, you can really start to develop your taste and imagination. Be your own critic but never stop trying out new ideas. And have fun!

$\mathcal{S}$OURCES AND SUPPLIERS

No source list can be complete, but here are the names of suppliers I have gathered that may be useful in pillow making. Though all the sources listed below were around when this book went to press, bear in mind that firms come and go. Many of the following fabric companies have showrooms across the country, so call the number listed for the showroom or store nearest to you.

FABRIC SOURCES

WHOLESALE OR TO-THE-TRADE

These showrooms sell to the trade, which means you can purchase through an architect or designer. Many of the firms have show- rooms throughout the country and sell trimming and wall covering as well as fabric.

ROBERT ALLEN
FABRICS
979 Third Avenue
New York, NY 10022
(212) 759-6660

BOUSSAC
979 Third Avenue
New York, NY 10022
(212) 421-0534

BRUNSCHWIG & FILS
979 Third Avenue
New York, NY 10022
(212) 838-7878

MANUEL CANOVAS
979 Third Avenue
New York, NY 10022
(212) 752-9588

CARLETON V
979 Third Avenue
New York, NY 10022
(212) 355-4525

CLARENCE HOUSE
211 East 58th Street
New York, NY 10022
(212) 752-2890

COWTAN & TOUT
979 Third Avenue
New York, NY 10022
(212) 753-4488

ROSE CUMMING, LTD.
232 East 59th Street
New York, NY 10022
(212) 758-0844

DECORATOR'S WALK
Fabric Gallery
160 East 56th Street
New York, NY 10022
(212) 355-5300
Office and Warehouse:
245 Newtown Road
Plain View, NY 11803
(516) 249-3100

DONGHIA
979 Third Avenue
New York, NY 10022
(212) 935-3713

EAGLESHAM PRINTS
979 Third Avenue
New York, NY 10022
(212) 759-2060

FONTHILL
979 Third Avenue
New York, NY 10022
(212) 924-3000

PHILIP GRAF
WALLPAPERS, INC.
979 Third Avenue
New York, NY 10022
(212) 755-1448

GREEF FABRICS, INC.
155 East 56th Street
New York, NY 10022
(212) 824-6200

HINSON & CO.
979 Third Avenue
New York, NY 10022
(212) 475-4100

JACK LENOR LARSEN
232 East 59th Street
New York, NY 10003
(212) 674-3993

LEE-JOFA, INC.
979 Third Avenue
New York, NY 10022
(212) 688-0444

OSBORNE & LITTLE
979 Third Avenue
New York, NY 10022
(212) 751-3333

PIERRE DEUX FABRICS
870 Madison Avenue
New York, NY 10022
(212) 570-9343

RANDOLPH & HEIN
101 Henry Adams Street
Galleria Design Center
Suite 101
San Francisco, CA 94107
(415) 864-3550

QUADRILLE
979 Third Avenue
New York, NY 10022
(212) 753-2995

SCALAMANDRE
942 Third Avenue
New York, NY 10022
(212) 980-3888
(See SILK SURPLUS for
retail division.)

F. SCHUMACHER & CO.
939 Third Avenue
New York, NY 10022
(212) 415-3900
(See WAVERLY FAB-
RICS for retail division.)

SONIA'S PLACE
979 Third Avenue
New York, NY 10022
(212) 355-5211

STROHEIM &
ROMANN, INC.
155 East 56th Street
New York, NY 10022
(212) 486-1500

WOODSON
979 Third Avenue
New York, NY 10022
(212) 684-0330

RETAIL: REGULAR FABRIC STORES

LAURA ASHLEY
(212) 735-5030
Stores nationwide provid-
ing fabrics, household
linens, and decorative
accessories.

BERGAMO FABRICS
37-20 34th Street
Long Island City, NY
11101
(718) 392-5000

THE FABRIC PLACE
136 Howard Street
Framingham, MA 01701
(617) 620-1030
Large range of decorative
and fashion fabrics; custom
drapery and upholstery.

FAR EASTERN FABRICS
171 Madison Avenue
New York, NY 10016
(212) 683-2623

RALPH LAUREN HOME
COLLECTION
Call (212) 642-8700 for an
up-to-date listing.

PIERRE DEUX FABRICS
870 Madison Avenue
New York, NY 10022
(212) 570-9343

POLI FABRICS
132 West 57th Street
New York, NY 10019
(212) 245-7589

SEAPORT FABRICS
Route 27
Mystic, CT 06355
(203) 536-8668
Home decorating fabrics at
a fraction of the regular
retail price.

SILK SURPLUS
235 East 58th Street
New York, NY 10022
(212) 753-6511
Retail showroom for Scalamandre, selling fabric and
trims.

VERMONT COUNTRY
STORE
Route 100
Weston, VT 05161
(802) 362-2400
A wide selection of fabrics
with a country flavor, such
as checks and calicos.

WAVERLY FABRICS, A
DIVISION OF F.
SCHUMACHER & CO.
79 Madison Avenue
New York, NY 10016
(212) 231-7900
Call (212) 704-9900 for
store locations. This is the
retail division of Schu-
macher decorative fabrics.

WOLFMAN•GOLD &
GOOD COMPANY
116 Greene Street
New York, NY 10012
(212) 431-1888
Household fabrics, cotton
damask, and lace, as well as
household pottery and pine
country furniture.

ANTIQUES SHOPS

Most areas have antiques
shops that carry the occa-
sional piece of fabric, vintage linen, or lace. You
probably have your favorite
sources. Here is a list ranging from spaces in department and specialty stores to
full-scale antiques shops.
Don't forget to peruse
street stalls, such as the
market on Manhattan's
Sixth Avenue at 26th
Street, and flea markets.

ANICHINI GALLERY
150 Fifth Avenue
New York, NY 10010
(212) 633-0788
Antique linens.

ANTIQUE TEXTILE
COMPANY
100 Portland Road
London, England
Antique fabrics and
clothing.

BARNEY'S, NEW YORK
61 Madison Avenue
New York, NY 10022
(212) 339-7300
This clothing specialty
store carries a selection of
antique linens.

BERGDORF
GOODMAN
754 Fifth Avenue
New York, NY 10019
(212) 753-7300
This department store
carries a selection of
antique linens.

FRED BRUNS
559 Hampton Road
Southampton, NY 11968
(516) 283-8097
Vintage household linens,
trimmings, lace, and
textiles.

CHERCHEZ
862 Lexington Avenue
New York, NY 10021
(212) 737-8215
This store specializing in
decorative accessories carries a selection of antique
linens.

COLLECTOR
ANTIQUES
3123 Magazine Street
New Orleans, LA 70115
(504) 897-0904
Antique linens.

DESCAMPS
723 Madison Avenue
New York, NY 10021
(212) 355-2522
Bed linens.

FANNY DOOLITTLE
ANTIQUES
157 Route 22
(at Route 311)
Patterson, NY 12563
(914) 878-6766
Has a selection of vintage
linens among other
antiques, including jewelry.

HOUSING WORKS
THRIFT SHOPS
Downtown:
143 West 17th Street
New York, NY 10011
(212) 366-0820
Uptown:
202 East 77th Street
New York, NY 10021
(212) 772-8461
Amazing finds of all kinds.

JANA STARR–JEAN
HOFFMAN ANTIQUES
236 East 80th Street
New York, NY 10021
(212) 535-6930
Antique bed and table
linens and laces, pillows,
lace panels, and lace
curtains.

LONDON LACE
167 Newbury Street
Boston, MA 02116
(617) 267-3506
Antique linens.

FRANÇOISE
NUNNALLÉ
By appointment only.
New York City
(212) 246-4281
Antique linens and lace;
large selection of decora-
tive antique tiebacks.

ELLEN O'NEILL
SUPPLY STORE
242 East 77th Street
New York, NY 10028
Antique linens, quilts, Mar-
seilles cloth bedspreads,
blankets, and fabrics.

REGINA LINENS
3369 Sacramento Street
San Francisco, CA 94118
(415) 563-8158
Antique linens.

ST. REMY
818 Lexington Avenue
New York, NY 10021
(212) 486-2018

THE VICTORIAN
GARDEN
136-58 72d Avenue
Kew Gardens, NY 11367
(718) 544-1657
Antique linens.

LILLIAN WILLIAMS
5 East 75th Street
New York, NY 10021
(212) 288-0488
Antique fabric.

AUCTIONS

WILLIAM DOYLE
GALLERIES
175 East 80th Street
New York, NY 10218
(212) 427-2730
Auctioneers and appraisers
who have auctions of cou-
ture, antique clothing, textiles, accessories, and
costume jewelry.

TRIMMING SUPPLIERS

Craft and fabric stores have
selections of ribbons and
trimmings. Decorative
trimmings can sometimes
be found in upholstery
supply shops, while all-
purpose decor stores like
Home Depot and Ikea are
across the country and sell
useful products. Look in
your local telephone Yel-
low Pages for those nearest
to you.

   In the garment district in
New York—which is west
of Fifth Avenue from 34th
Street up to 40th Street—
there are many small sup-
ply shops that sell mainly
to the trade at wholesale
prices. Other cities in
which there is a garment
district or decorative-trades
area usually have stores
that sell notions, ribbons,
and trimmings to the trade.
However, many of these
shops are willing to sell to
off-the-street customers at
retail prices.

   Many of the large decorator fabric houses carry a
line of passementerie that
can range from simple
tapes to very elaborate and
very expensive confections.

BRUNSCHWIG & FILS
979 Third Avenue
New York, NY 10022
(212) 838-7878
Showrooms worldwide
carry decorative passe-
menterie as well as fabric
and wall covering.

CLARENCE HOUSE
211 East 58th Street
New York, NY 10022
(212) 752-2890
Showrooms nationwide
carry decorative passe-
menterie as well as fabric
and wall covering.

CONSO PRODUCTS
COMPANY (Division
of Springs Industries)
295 Fifth Avenue
New York, NY 10036
(212) 686-7676
Big range of cotton cords
and ropes, straight, bullion,
and bobble fringes, and
tassels.

THE GROUND FLOOR
95 Broad Street
Charleston SC 29401
(803) 722-1838
Tassels and pulls for curtains in a variety of styles
that can be colored to go
with fabric.

HYMAN HENDLER
& SONS
67 West 38th Street
New York, NY 10018
(212) 840-8393
Huge selection of ribbons
including many interesting
small amounts of vintage
ribbons and trimmings.

LEE-JOFA, INC.
979 Third Avenue
New York, NY 10022
(212) 688-0444
Showrooms nationwide
carry decorative passe-
menterie as well as fabric
and wallpaper.

PASSEMENTERIE INC.
39-14 Crescent Street
Long Island City, NY
11101
(212) 643-8899
and (718) 392-0100
Decorative trimmings.

SCALAMANDRE
950 Third Avenue
New York, NY 10022
(212) 980-3888
Showrooms nationwide
carry decorative passe-
menterie as well as fabric.

SOGOOD INC.
28 West 38th Street
New York, NY 10018
(212) 398-0236
Big selection of ribbon,
especially grosgrains in
many widths and colors;
will sell retail.

SEWING EQUIPMENT SUPPLIERS

Most cities and towns have
handicraft shops where a
variety of sewing equip-
ment and supplies can be
bought. If you live in an
isolated area, it is a good
idea to have mail-order cat-
alogs. The names of these
suppliers may be useful.

ATLANTIC FEATHER
AND FOAM
330 Morgan Avenue
Brooklyn, NY 11211
(718) 782-4300
Pillow forms in custom
sizes and in a variety of
fillings.

COATS & CLARK, INC.
Department CS
PO Box 1010
Toccoa, GA 30577
Threads and notions such
as bias tape, fillers, inter-
facing, and zippers.

THE D.M.C.
CORPORATION
107 Trumbull Street
Elizabeth, NJ 07206
(908) 351-4550
Threads for embroidery.

ERICA WILSON
NEEDLE WORKS
717 Madison Avenue
New York, NY 10022
(212) 838-7290
Yarns and canvas for
needlepoint and
embroidery.

NEW YORK NOTION
CO. OF CHICAGO
2040 North Janice Avenue
Melrose Park, IL 60160
Send for free catalog of
notions.

OFFRAY RIBBONS
Route 24
PO Box 601
Chester, NJ 07930
(908) 879-4700

TALON, INC.
335 West 35th Street
New York, NY 10001
(212) 564-6300
Zippers.

TOTAL SEWING, INC.
PO Box 438
3729 Grand Boulevard
Brookfield, IL 60513
Send for free catalog.

WOOLWORKS INC.
838 Madison Avenue or
1260 Third Avenue
New York, NY 10021
(212) 861-8700
Yarns and canvas for
needlepoint.

TEXTILE REPAIRS

BETTY LA CASSE
37 Prescott Avenue
White Plains, NY 10605
(914) 948-7573
Repairs and restores fine
fabrics, including cash-
mere; specializes in lace.

GINA BIANCO
Call (718) 788-1211 for
appointment. Restores
any fabric; textile conserva-
tionist.

EVELYN KENNEDY
SEWTIQUE
391 Long Hill Road
Groton, CT 06340-1293
(203) 445-7320
Restores vintage and con-
temporary textiles, including beading, furs, lace,
leather; licensed by the
International Society of
Appraisers.

THE LAUNDRY AT
LINENS LIMITED
240 N. Milwaukee Street
Milwaukee, WI 53202
(414) 223-1123
(800) 637-6334 for infor-
mation, brochures, price
lists; restoration service for
fine table linen, needle-
point, wedding veils, christening gowns, and more.

CAROLYN NIEZGODA
2376 Eighty-fourth St.
Brooklyn, NY 11214
(718) 946-6652
Restores, refurbishes,
designs accessories for
wedding and christening
gowns; archival cleaning.

GLOSSARY OF TERMS

Very few glossaries dealing with textiles can be complete because there are thousands of fabrics. Fabrics and names change continually because of innovative technology. Here are some fabrics and terms that are useful in the craft of making pillows.

all over A term for a printed fabric that is quite densely covered with a small repeating design.

antique rugs Small pieces of worn antique rugs, especially those from the Middle East, are often used to make pillows.

appliqué A type of embroidery whereby one fabric is cut into a shape and "applied" or sewn to another fabric to form a decoration. Decorative stitches may be used both in the application and on top of the applied motif. There are some commercial appliqués with adhesive backing that can be attached with a hot iron, but these are often unrefined in color and design and used primarily for children's clothes.

arabesque A curving design of the late eighteenth and early nineteenth centuries, inspired by Roman murals. Arabesques showed airy, interlaced patterns using classical figures, urns, medalions, and acanthus leaves.

batik The technique of batik originated in Java and is one of the oldest forms of dying cotton. Portions of cloth are treated with wax so that only the areas not covered in wax will be dyed. Batiks can be complex, requiring several different waxings and dippings in varying colors. The final result has a pleasing mottled and streaked effect, at its best in genuine handmade fabric from the Far East. Nowadays printing machines imitate the hand-dyed effect. (See *wax print.*)

beading Many antique needlepoint pieces were worked with tiny glass beads. These make wonderful pillows. To repair damaged beading, use beading needles, which are very fine, and glass beads from craft shops.

bias The true bias is at a 45-degree angle from the selvedge.

bias binding or bias tape Fabric cut into narrow strips on the bias with the raw edges folded in, used for trimming and binding. Bias binding can be bought prepackaged in a variety of colors and in several widths. It can also be made by hand.

braid Decorative trimming that can be topstitched or hand-sewn to decorate, or to outline the focal part of a pillow or hide a seam. Braids come up to 4 inches (10 cm) wide and in many weaves and colors.

brocaded fabric Brocading is a weaving process, though fabrics are often inaccurately called brocades. Usually—but not exclusively—brocaded fabrics are made of silk or metal threads, woven in an elaborate technique that creates an embroidered effect. A small, precious piece of brocaded fabric can be mounted on silk taffeta to make a very beautiful pillow. (See *lampas.*)

calico An inexpensive cotton fabric that originated in Calcutta, India, with a resist-printed (also called "discharge-printed") background, covered in simple, small-scale designs in two or three colors. Designs can be tiny, simple flowers or geometrics, and have a distinctively naive, American country look.

cambric A soft, closely woven cotton fabric, usually white, with a calendered, glossy finish. It can be used to back lightweight fabrics and, if the weave is dense enough, in place of ticking for pillow casings. The name comes from Cambrai, France, where it was originally made of linen and used for table and church linen.

canvas A heavy, strong cotton or linen (see *duck*); also an open-mesh fabric that comes in various qualities used for needlepoint embroidery; also an unbleached linen canvas used as interfacing in tailoring.

"centering" Establishing the focal part of a printed pattern before cutting a pillow.

chambray A cotton shirting, also named after the French town Cambrai, where it was originally made. It can be used in the same way as cambric.

chenille A fabric—woven or knitted—made using chenille yarn, which is fuzzy like a caterpillar (from the French word for *caterpillar*).

chicken feathers and down A type of stuffing for pillows that is a notch below goose feathers and down.

chiné Though the French word originally meant "made Chinese," the term now refers to fine silk warp-dyed fabrics.

chino Any one of a variety of cotton or cotton-blend fabrics resembling army twill, usually dyed khaki or beige. Suitable for casual pillows in a boy's room or a weekend retreat.

chintz Derived from a Hindu word, chintz is printed cotton fabric, often with a glazed finish, used

almost exclusively in interior decoration.

compound weaves Fabrics with more than one warp and more than one filling. Some, such as brocaded ottoman, or a combination of damask and brocading, can be complex, requiring many days just to set up the loom.

conversationals Prints that are amusing, show specific themes, or are idiosyncratic.

cord Twisted or braided fibers in any of a number of sizes and variations, either applied to or inserted into upholstery and onto pillow edges to add color and definition. When cord is made more than 1 inch (3 cm) in diameter it is referred to as rope.

corduroy Any one of many variations of velvety-pile fabrics woven into vertical ribs, or wales, and then cut. Corduroy is useful for sporty pillows or pillows in a boy's room. Uncut corduroy has a ribless pile and can be useful as a modest velveteen. (From the French *corde du roi*—originally it was made for the king.)

crewel Designs based on a certain type of late-seventeenth-century English embroidery using wool on unbleached linen or cotton. The patterns usually combine leaves, vines, flowers, and animals. Pillows can be embroidered to resemble crewelwork.

cushion British and American haut décor term for a "throw pillow" tossed on furniture; many Americans use the term *cushion* for a thick seat pad on upholstered sofas and armchairs. (See *pillow.*)

damask A fabric named after the Syrian city of Damascus, center of the textile trades between the East and the West in the thirteenth century. It was brought to the Western world by Marco Polo. Damask, a firm, glossy fabric with a figured weave somewhat similar to a brocade weave, is created by combining two weaves, twill and satin. Check it by seeing if the reverse has satin in the place of twill, and twill in the place of satin. Damask is reversible and limited to two colors—the warp and the weft threads. It is now produced on mechanized Jacquard looms.

denim A rugged work clothes fabric with a twill weave, usually in a shade of blue. The names derives from "de Nîmes"—of Nîmes in France—where the cloth was first made. Good for making pillows for a sporty, country, or ranch-style room. Clothing made from denim can be cut up and used for pillows.

dimity A fairly lightweight, unpretentious fabric usually with vertical ribs. Furnishing-weight dimity makes good-looking solid pillows with a slight texture.

district check A houndstooth check with a larger, contrasting check dividing it (named by local Scottish tweed makers).

dobby A weave requiring special loom adjustments to produce small, symmetrical, repeating motifs. Named for the English "dobby boy," who sat on top of the loom and lifted the warp threads (from *dobbin,* a term for a workhorse).

"dressing down" A term often used for smoothing down curtains that have just been hung, but I use it in pillow making to mean the process of fluffing up and smoothing out the pillow and spreading the stuffing.

duck Firm, durable, heavy cotton or cotton blend in a plain weave that comes in many colors and weights. Useful for casual pillows. (See *canvas.*)

dupion Slubbed silk formed from double cocoons called dupions. Good for pillows in a formal room.

edgestitch A seamstress's term for machine stitching as close to the edge of a piece of fabric, or on a seam, as possible. It can be a holding, or decorative stitch.

eiderdown The most luxurious and costly stuffing for pillows, down from the eider.

embossing A design pressed into fabric with heat, rather like making a waffle. (See *gaufrage.*)

embroidery Many ways of embellishing fabric with applied colored or white thread. Some of the types are *appliqué, beadwork, crewel, cutwork, drawn work* (also called *hemstitching* or *fagoting*), *eyelet embroidery* (called *broderie anglaise* in England and France), *needlepoint* (see also *gros point* and *petit point*), *quilting, smocking, stump work* (the name given to a padded, dimensional embroidery done since Elizabethan times. In the nineteenth century a variation of the technique became called *Berlin work* as it was a popular craft among German ladies).

Surface stitches include the *backstitch, chain* stitch, *French knots, herringbone* stitch, *lazy daisy, satin* stitch, and more. Originally done

by hand, nowadays many embroidered designs are made on a schiffli or other type of machine.

felt A fabric formed by matting fibers—usually wool or wool blend—under heat and pressure. Felt comes in many colors and several weights and is useful for appliqué as the cut edges do not fray.

fiberfill Polyester stuffing that can be bought in various forms, such as in sheets to use in quilts and seat pads, in small pieces to stuff into pillows, or in pillow forms.

filler cord Tubular cotton cord used to make piping or welting. Filler cord comes in widths from $\frac{1}{8}$ inch to 1 inch (3 mm to 2.5 cm) in diameter.

flannel A soft fabric of cotton or wool or a blend that is napped on one or both sides. In an off-white raw state it is used as interlining and is useful to stuff seat pads.

flounce An embroidered border design.

French corners Gathering or pleating at the corners of cushions and pillows to give a soft, rounded effect. Furniture makers use the terms *butterfly corners, gathered corners,* and sometimes *Turkish corners.*

fringe A decorative trimming made up of cut, looped, or knotted threads hanging from a heading. Varieties include:

Ball fringe: Sometimes called bobble fringe, this is made by clustering fringe yarns which are then steamed to form balls.

Beaded fringe: Used mostly on curtains, beaded fringes can be effective also on pillows. They can be found made with colorless crystal-looking beads, translucent colored beads, wood beads, and jetlike beads.

Block fringe: Fringe made in recurring blocks of color.

Bullion fringe: Heavy fringe made from twisted yarns that double back on themselves, forming a ropelike effect. Because of the scale, use only on large pillows.

Fan-edged fringe: Also called *giselle,* fan edging is a supple, silky type of block fringe, but has a soft zigzag edge formed from loops.

Knotted fringe: Long fringe—from 3 inches to 12 inches (8 cm to 30 cm)—whereby yarns are clumped together and knotted in various decorative ways. The best are hand-knotted, but there are many machine-made versions.

Moss fringe: Sometimes called *brush* fringe, moss fringe is a full, thick, silky, straight-cut fringe, usually no wider than 1 inch (2.5 cm) and usually inserted into a seam so the beading does not show. It often looks most effective when the fringe is doubled and therefore fuller.

*Self-*fringe: If the fabric you are using is suitable, you can pull threads out to make your own fringe.

Tassel fringe: Fringe formed from small tassels.

gathering A term for pulling fabric along a line of stitching so that it puckers to give fullness; also called *shirring.*

gaufrage   A process of embossing fabric with a heated weight to create a pattern, from the Flemish for *waffle.* (See *embossing.*)

gimp   A flat, narrow (usually ⅜ inch to ½ inch [1 cm to 13 mm] wide) woven trimming that comes in a variety of raised patterns; used in many ways in interior decoration and especially useful as a trimming on pillows.

gingham   Usually made of cotton or cotton and synthetic (but can be silk), ginghams are woven to have a block or checkered effect. Ginghams come in many colors and sizes, and are readily available in fabric stores. Pillows made of gingham tend to have a casual country look.

glazed   A term used to describe a glossy fabric surface, produced by heat, heavy pressure, chemical action, or a glazing substance. Chintz, for instance, is usually glazed.

goose down   Next to eiderdown, the most luxurious pillow stuffing.

grain   The true warp or the direction of vertical threads of a fabric. Cross grain is the direction of the weft or horizontal threads. Bias is the diagonal direction that is at a 45-degree angle to the selvedge; "on the cross" is another term for the bias direction.

grosgrain   Grosgrain is a fine, cross-ribbed fabric. It is also a ribbed ribbon that comes in many sizes and colors, and is very useful in pillow making.

gros point and **petit point**   Needlework stitches, large and small. They can both be imitated on decorative fabrics, which are useful to use as framing or backs for fancy handmade needlepoint pillows.

gusset   An insert or side piece that gives shape or dimension. Gussets are used in dressmaking (often to make the underarm of a sleeve fit better, or on gloves between each finger. On pillows they are usually side pieces to give height.

herringbone   A weave in which twills, or diagonal weaves, alternate directions, forming a zigzag pattern like a herring's backbone, sometimes called a chevron weave.

horsehair   A cloth used extensively in the eighteenth and nineteenth centuries for upholstery. The weft is made of hair from horses' tails, therefore real horsehair fabric is only about 21 inches (53 cm) wide. Now synthetic horsehair is available in standard widths. Horsehair is not comfortable for pillows, but is hard wearing as a seat pad.

ikat   Warp-dyed fabrics originally from Indonesia, India, and Afghanistan. The warp is printed or tie-dyed before weaving.

imberline   A complex fabric with a woven, striped ground and a large damask pattern, used since the eighteenth century for upholstery and wall hangings. Handsome pillows can be made by centering them on the imberline's design.

Jacquard   Method of weaving large-patterned designs by using punched cards, thus saving hand labor. Named after the Frenchman Joseph-Marie Jacquard (1752–

1834). Jacquard fabrics are those woven on a Jacquard loom.

kapok   From a Malaysian tree, a mass of silky fibers used as pillow or mattress filling or for insulation.

knife edge   A term used to describe seat pads and pillows with no insert, gusset, or gathers at the corners of fabric to add dimension to the shape.

lace   Fine openwork fabric or edging often made from thread, or cut and embroidered. There are many varieties, each with their own characteristics:

Point lace, made from thread by needle, such as *Alençon* lace, *guipure,* and *Venise* lace

Pillow lace, made on a pillow using bobbins, such as *Chantilly* lace, *Cluny* lace, *Nottingham* lace, and *Val* (Valenciennes) lace

Crocheted lace, such as *Irish* lace

Lace made with woven ribbons, such as *Renaissance* lace

Lace appliquéd to net, such as *Brussels* lace, and *Normandy* lace

Schiffli embroidery, which originated in Switzerland (schiffli means "boat" and refers to a boat-shaped shuttle on the schiffli machine). A lacy effect is produced by embroidering motifs on a net ground

Lace darned in squares onto a mesh ground, such as *filet* lace

Tatting, which makes fine, spiderweb effects from thread worked by hand with a special double-pointed bobbin.

ladder stitch A hand-done stitch for sewing up the final opening to finish a pillow; also called a slip stitch (see Diagram 20 on page 36).

lambrequin A French word used to describe a framing shape like curtains on a proscenium opening.

lamé A fabric made with metallic thread or synthetic metallic thread.

lampas A compound woven cloth with figured patterns, bulkier than a true brocaded cloth because all the additional wefts are bound into the fabric and carried from selvedge to selvedge. (See *brocaded fabric.*)

leather Often used as a term for all animal skin. Leather can be printed, embossed, dyed, sueded, cut and woven, fringed, made into patchwork, etc. Often what we call suede is brushed cowhide, though real suede is softer and comes in smaller skins.

looseback Refers to soft, upholstered furniture with separately made seat back cushions. (Tightback furniture has cushioning built into the back.)

macaron A passementerie term for a flat, buttonlike decorative motif usually covered in silk thread. *Macarons* are named after the almond-flavored Italian cookie.

madras A fine, hand-loomed cotton, named after the town in India, that comes in plain, checked, or striped variations. The vegetable dyes, especially indigo, are guaranteed to "bleed," which is considered an advantage. There are many domestic imitations that are waterfast. Madras pillows work well in a casual room.

matelassé A double-woven Jacquard fabric with a quilted or ruched appearance.

mohair velvet Velvet with pile made from the shearings of angora goats.

moiré Fabric with a watered-silk appearance. Originally produced by applying uneven pressure from heated cylinders to a finely ribbed silk; now available in woven or printed versions.

muslin Muslin is a term used for a variety of simple cotton fabrics. Most often it is a natural-colored, unbleached, relatively inexpensive cotton sheeting used to make *toiles,* or draped patterns for clothing (not to be confused with toile de Jouy, a painted cloth; see *toile.*). Muslin is useful as a backing fabric, as the covering for a pillow form, or as inexpensive fabric to try out an experimental pillow pattern. Muslin comes in light, medium, and heavy weights.

nap The way fibers on the face of goods are raised or teased up to make a fabric softer, warmer, or denser. Nap influences the direction in which fabric is cut to give a lighter or darker effect, as does pile. (See *pile.*)

needle board A device used for pressing velvet without bruising the pile. Fine metal spikes are set into a flat, flexible pad which is placed on a regular ironing board.

needlepoint There are many variations on the art of needlepoint embroidery, which is most often— but not only—worked with wool yarns in formations on open-weave canvas to form pictures or abstract designs. Stitches include *bargello, petit point, gros point,* and combinations with beading.

ombré A shaded effect (French for *shadowed*).

one way A printed pattern that can be cut only in one direction.

ottoman A fabric used in interior decoration with silky ribs that run from selvedge to selvedge. The hidden insides of the ribs are often of cotton; the surface can be silk or some other fiber with a sheen. Ottoman comes in ribs of various sizes, usually from $\frac{1}{10}$ inch to $\frac{1}{4}$ inch (2.5 mm to 6.4 mm) wide, and in many colors. Ottoman is a particularly useful fabric for pillow making: as a frame, as backing, and as piping fabric. An ottoman is also a large, padded footstool often used with an upholstered armchair.

paisley A design based on the Indian cone motif, named after Paisley in Scotland, where soft wool shawls using variations of these patterns were produced to copy the more expensive originals made in Kashmir, India.

passementerie Any type of cord, braid, or fringe used for embellishment. Can range from a simple edging to an elaborate handmade confection.

patchwork Any number of variations joining small pieces of fabric together to produce a larger piece of cloth. Sometimes the pieces are sewn randomly, and sometimes they form intricate arrangements with specific names. Patchwork is often quilted and patchwork names are associated with quilts, such as: *Basket or Flowerpot; crazy* quilts, which are random patches feather-stitched at the seams; *coffin* quilts, which often combined appliqué and patchwork and commemorated those who had died; *Double Square; Eccentric Star; Friendship,* often with appliqués of hands; *Joseph's Coat; Log Cabin; Mariner's Compass; Nine Patch; Pinwheel; Princess Feather; Rocky Road; Sawtooth; Schoolhouse; Star of Bethlehem;* and *Wild Goose Chase.* Six- or eight-sided patchwork is a variation in which fabric is basted onto cardboard forms, then overstitched together on the wrong side; then the cardboard is removed. *Yo-yo* patchwork is made of small circles of fabric that are gathered around the edges, pulled tight, and hand-stitched together at the top, bottom, and sides, so that the patchwork forms spaces between the circles (see the left photograph on page 26). When the circles are puffed out with padding, they are called *puffs.*

patina   In fabrics, an antiqued look, sometimes achieved through age and sometimes contrived.

pile   The way various yarns project from a foundation fabric. Piles may be cut, as in velvet, or uncut, as in terry cloth. (See *nap.*)

pillow   See *cushion.*

piping   Fabric cut in bias strips, filled with cording, and then stitched between seams to give contrast or emphasis to the edges of pillows, slipcovers, or upholstery. Also known as welting. "Self-piping" is the term used when the fabric and the piping match. (See *welt.*)

piqué   A dobby woven fabric, most distinctively of white cotton, that comes in a variety of surface weaves—fine, medium, and wide wale ribs, bird's eye, bull's eye, diamond, honeycomb, waffle, and other patterns. Piqué has a crisp appearance and can make good-looking pillows for a bed or for an all-white room.

plaid   A pattern formed by stripes in the warp and the weft. The name comes from the Scottish "plaid" which was a long, wide scarf worn over one shoulder. (See *tartan.*)

platform   The horizontal area of a chair or sofa that seat pads or cushions sit on.

pleats   Fabric that is folded and stitched—and often pressed—in a regular progression to control fullness. Types of pleats include:

Accordion pleats: A simple up-and-down pressed fold like the pleats in an accordion box.

Box pleats: Pleats that alternately change direction, forming boxlike pleats on the right side, and inverted pleats or separated inverted pleats on the wrong side.

Crystal pleats: Tiny, even accordion pleats.

Inverted pleats: Two or more pleats that change direction, meeting to form a V formation at the top where they are secured. A series of inverted pleats may form box pleats or spread-out box pleats on the reverse.

Knife edge pleats: A series of one way pleats, usually pressed.

Pinch pleats: Pleats bunched up into groups, or a series of single bunched-up pleats. These are usually found at the top of curtains, designed to control the fullness of the fabric, and can be made by applying commercially made curtain tape and hooks or can be hand-sewn.

Sunray pleats: Accordion pleats that start small and grow wider, disregarding the grain of the fabric.

Unpressed pleats: Any box, inverted, or knife pleats secured at the top but left unpressed to form soft folds.

pongee   Usually refers to a type of unbleached, plain-weave silk. Simple pillows of pongee can be elegant in a room of neutral colors and textures.

quilt   Quilting is the technique of stitching two fabrics together with a batting between for warmth and to add dimension to the design. In the past, quilts were often made from previously stitched and embellished patchwork, and the top, batting, and lining were assembled at a quilting bee, using a special frame.

railroading   A method by which goods are cut down the grain as opposed to the orthodox method of cutting across the grain (which necessitates matching the print on each seam). Railroading is useful for nondirectional fabrics to save needless seams, especially on a long seat pad for a banquette.

repeat   The length of a printed or woven pattern before it repeats itself. A large repeat is always more expensive to use because more cloth is required to match the print.

ribbon Ribbons come in many shapes, colors, sizes, weaves, and fibers. Regular ribbon sizes are referred to by numbers in the trade, ranging from #1, ¼ inch (7 mm), to #40, 3 inch (8 cm). Specialty ribbons can be even wider. Types of ribbon include *grosgrain* ribbon; *Jacquard* ribbon; *picot-edged* ribbon, which has a tiny loop spaced along each selvedge and gives a nice old-fashioned effect; *satin weave* ribbon—some are single-faced with the satin effect on only one side, but the best quality are double-faced with satin weave on both sides; *taffeta weave* ribbon; *velvet* ribbon; and *combinations* of all of these varieties. Ribbons can be used as trimming—topstitched on like a braid, or gathered to form a small ruffle—or they can be woven to make pillows.

rickrack A thin, flat braid that forms zigzags. Be cautious using rickrack because it comes in unsubtle colors and tends to have a cheapening, kitchen-y effect.

right-angled ruler A metal ruler 16 inches (approximately 40 cm) in one direction with a ruler 24 inches (approximately 61 cm) long at right angles to it.

rope See *cord.*

rosette A decorative, circular confection made of fabric or ribbon, used usually to punctuate draperies, but can decorate a pillow. A motif with a similar use is a square or Maltese cross concocted from ribbon or fabric.

ruche A strip of material used for trimming that has been gathered on both edges, such as a ruched piping or a ruched gusset.

rugs Many varieties of rugs, especially antique ones from the Middle East, can be used to make cushions. As they are often too thick to sew on a machine, much of the work has to be hand-sewn.

sateen A fabric in a satin weave, usually made of mercerized cotton with a lustrous but less gleamingly shiny look than silk satin. It can therefore be used much more informally than satin.

satin A weave with a warp of the most precious threads, such as silk, that covers the weft in order to produce a reflective, lustrous effect. Satin can be made of different fibers but the most luxurious is silk, which reflects light and takes color brilliantly. *Slipper* satin is heavy and somewhat stiff. *Upholstery* satin is of a heavy weight, has a cotton back, and tends to curl back on itself when being cut, but is a wonderful material for glamorous pillows. (See *weaves.*)

seat pad Pads of varying thickness used to soften a chair seat or to protect a cane seat. Sometimes these are called squabs in England.

self-fabric Matching fabric, such as for piping, cut from the same cloth as the pillow.

selvedge The woven edges of a piece of cloth. On a printed decorative fabric this is where you often find the name of the company that created it, a color key indicating the number of colors used to print it, and arrows indicating the up-and-down direction of its design.

sham A pillow cover that can be slipped off and on easily by means of an overlapping back. These may sometimes be closed by buttons or ribbonlike ties.

shantung Slubbed silk, often unbleached but also found in colors. Heavy shantung makes good large "background" pillows to use at either end of a sofa.

shears A large-bladed pair of scissors used for cutting fabric.

slub When fibers vary from thin to thick this is called a slub. Slubs create texture in the weave.

soutache A narrow braid, originally used on military uniforms, usually topstitched on in a central groove.

squab An old English term for a removable seat pad on a chair.

stitches (hand) There are many variations of hand stitches used in plain sewing. Here are a few:

Backstitch: This is a strong stitch that gives the effect of a continuous line. The needle goes in and out, then is put back to where the first stitch entered, and is brought out the width of two stitches beyond; then the process is repeated.

Blanket stitch: A spaced edging stitch useful as a decorative hem.

Buttonhole stitch: A close, tighter stitch than the blanket stitch for hand-stitching buttonholes, also used in eyelet embroidery.

Ladder stitch: Also called *blind* stitch or *slip* stitch. (See *ladder stitch* entry and Diagram 20 on page 36.)

Running stitch: This is the simplest of all stitches. The needle enters in and out and repeats in even spaces. *Embroidery* stitches (see *embroidery*) are for decoration rather than use.

strié A fine, uneven vertical stripe. The French term *strié* is used to describe a printed cloth with irregular, tone-on-tone streaks, as if liquid had been dripped on it. The same term is used for wallpaper with the same effect.

stripes Parallel lines printed or woven on textiles in many variations. Striped fabrics are useful in making pillows because they can be imaginatively cut and pieced to form unique designs.

suede Fine leather with a napped surface that makes luxurious pillows. Brushed cowhide is a coarser, more sporty, and less expensive form of suede. Suede cloth is a fabric with a napped surface that imitates suede. It is easier to cut and sew and is less expensive than real suede, but lacks real suede's glamour.

tabby The simplest over-and-under weave, such as children use to make pot holders in kindergarten; also called a *plain weave.*

taffeta We tend to think of taffeta as a crisp, silklike fabric, but it is really a weave. Taffeta comes in many colors and makes wonderful, light, luxurious pillows. Cotton taffeta is also useful for less formal pillows. Some variations of taffeta include:

Antique taffeta, which has a slubbed texture.

Shot taffeta, which has one color yarn in the warp and another in the weft, which gives an iridescent effect.

Faille taffeta, which has a heavy weight and a distinct ribbed effect.

Moiré taffeta, which has a heat-pressed watered effect.

Paper taffeta, which is lightweight with a crisp finish like paper, useful for making double frills with pinked edges.

tartan Usually wool or worsted cloth, but can be cotton, woven in multicolored block and checked patterns based on those used in Scottish clans to make kilts. Pillows of tartan look good in a masculine room such as a study, library, or den. (See *plaid.*)

tassel A passementerie hanging ornament with a head, neck, and skirt formed of threads. Tassels can range from simple cotton ornaments to elaborate silk-covered confections.

tatting Delicate hand-done lace made from a single thread looped and knotted by means of a distinctive double-ended shuttle.

terry cloth A cotton toweling fabric made absorbent with a looped pile on one or both sides. Terry cloth can be bought by the yard to make pillows for a bathroom, or in the form of towels, which can be cut and made into pillows. Recycle worn towels using the best parts to make pillows or washable, inviting seat pads for a bathroom chair.

ticking Sometimes called mattress ticking, this fabric is compactly woven because it was originally used to cover mattresses and feather pillows. Now there are many imitations that are not so tightly woven. Most tickings have a white background with blue or brown woven railroad stripes, though other colors—black, red, pink—are made.

tightback Refers to soft, upholstered furniture in which the back cushioning is part of the piece. (Looseback means the cushions are separate and can be removed from the back.)

toile A monotone print with an intricate, engraved quality, often of a historical, pictorial subject. The name is short for toile de Jouy; Jouy is a town in France where many famous toiles were printed. Toiles make interesting pillows and usually do not require elaborate detailing because the print tells the story. Toile is also a name for muslin (see *muslin*).

trapunto A decorative, linear, quilted design made by stitching through two layers and trapping soft cotton cords underneath to form a pattern. Trapunto is a useful technique to give depth and pattern to a pillow made of solid cloth.

tufting A method of upholstering using buttons or decorative knots to hold the fabric covering the deep padding in place. Seat pads are often tufted. Sometimes pillows have a large covered button sewn through the center.

turk's head A globe-shaped, decorative, handmade knot formed from cord or fabric tubing, which can be used on the corners of pillows.

Turkish corners See *French corners.*

tussah A dry-feeling, rough type of silk with slubs from uncultivated silkworms. Large down-filled simple tussah pillows can look very elegant as a foil for fancier pillows.

twill A diagonal weave. Twills can be of cotton, wool, worsted, and various blends. Pillows of twill are somewhat masculine and sporty.

velvet There are many kinds of velvet made from a variety of fibers but they all have in common a cut pile which gives an appealing look and a soft hand. Velvet is particularly useful in pillow making. When it is hand painted it resembles the theorem paintings that were made in the nineteenth century. The king of velvets is silk velvet, the best being made in the French town of Lyon.

Here are some types that can be made into elegant pillows:

Antique velvet can be really old velvet or velvet that has been distressed to look older than it is.

Ciselé velvet is a combination of cut and uncut velvet (from the French for *sculptured* or *chiseled*).

Cut velvet is a term we tend to use indiscriminately because, technically, all velvet with a soft pile is "cut." Cut velvet is often used to describe voided velvet, which is woven to have some areas with pile and some with no pile.

Devoré velvet has a velvet pile on fine mesh with the pile burned away in areas to form three-dimensional patterns; used mainly for clothing, as it is rather fragile for most decorative uses.

Figured velvet is a patterned velvet with a design formed by cut and uncut loops.

Linen velvet is velvet with a linen pile which has a sheen and takes color especially well.

Mohair velvet is a plushy-looking velvet made from mohair fiber which comes from the angora goat. It is used mostly in decoration, and works well for pillows.

Panné velvet is a lightweight, lustrous silk or synthetic velvet with the pile laid flat in one direction. It has an antique look.

Pile on pile velvet has a sculptured appearance produced by weaving the velvet pile with two different heights.

Plush is a type of velvet with a pile more than $\frac{1}{8}$ inch (3 mm) high.

Single velvet: Nowadays most velvets are made double, then the fabric is split horizontally to form the pile. The pile on single velvet (also called *wire* velvet) is made by hand-weaving over slotted wires which are then hand-cut with a knife. (Two wonderful classic velvets made in France, and sold in America by Brunschwig & Fils, are single velvets woven into Jacquard designs inspired by tiger and leopard patterns. These velvets are still hand-woven and hand-cut laboriously, with only a few inches being produced each day. They are expensive but make glamorous pillows.)

Velour is similar to velveteen but with a higher cotton pile. Velour is also a knitted fabric used for sportswear, and should be used for pillows only in desperation.

Voided velvet is a Jacquard-patterned fabric with velvet pile areas contrasting with no-pile areas, giving a sculptured effect.

velveteen Also known as cotton velvet, velveteen comes in many colors and is durable as well as washable. It has a lower pile and less sheen and is less easily bruised than velvet. Velveteen is a versatile fabric for pillows because it can look both formal and casual. Use it to frame embroidery and to back pillows. Chosen in the nineteenth century to make theorem paintings, today velveteen is still the ideal cloth to use for painted pillows.

vermicelli Small, continuous curly lines in a design (from the Italian for *worms*). Vermicelli effects can be printed or embroidered.

warp The threads that run down a fabric. These threads are set up on a loom first, and the weft threads are then woven in. (See *weft.*)

warp-printing A method of printing in which first a pattern is printed, painted, or tie-dyed on the warp, and then a plain filler is woven in, producing a softened effect with a slightly fuzzy edge. The fabric, though printed, appears the same on both sides. (See *chiné* and *ikat.*)

wax print A fabric produced by applying wax in a pattern onto cloth, dipping the cloth into dye, and then removing the wax, leaving the original uncolored cloth beneath. Sometimes called *resist printing.* (See *batik.*)

weaves There have been no new basic weaves invented since 1747 when a book of weaves was published in Berlin, Germany. All weaves—simple, elaborate, or compound—are derived from three fundamental types:

Plain weave: A simple over and under rather like the technique we used to make pot holders in kindergarten (also called tabby weave, or one-up/one-down weave). Some plain weave fabrics are muslin, taffeta, voile, and sheeting.

Twill weave: A diagonal weave, usually at a 45-degree angle, but some can be steep, up to 75 degrees, or reclining, down to 15 degrees. Twilled cloths that slant to the right include cavalry twill,

covert, gabardine, serge, and whipcord. Left-hand twills include denim, and jean cloth, galatea, some drills, and some ticking cloths.

Satin weave: The surface is almost entirely filled up with warp, floating strands, giving a lustrous surface and a dull back. Satin fabrics include satin crepe, panne satin, upholstery satin, and slipper satin. (See *satin*.)

weft   The threads that weave across the warp from selvedge to selvedge; sometimes called the filling or the woof. (See *warp*.)

welt   Another term for piping. (See *piping*.)

yarn-dyed fabric   Fabric made from yarns dyed before they are made into cloth. Yarn-dyed fabrics are superior to piece-dyed fabric because the threads are completely and individually covered in dye.

yardstick   A 36-inch-long wooden stick marked like a ruler.

zipper foot   An sewing machine attachment that enables the needle to stitch right up close to a raised object such as a zipper or a piping. Some zipper feet can be adjusted to stitch to the right or to the left.

Index